VAN BUREN DISTRICT LIBRARY
DECATUR
W9-BMJ-109

Praise for *Liking the Child*

"Dr. Bernstein has written a wonderful book, helping parents learn new ways of thinking and behaving in order to solve the problems they have with their children. His strategies are practical and concrete and very useful. I highly recommend this book to parents (and professionals who work with parents). It's very empowering to learn that "the key to a good relationship with your child rests more with you than your child."
  —JUDITH S. BECK, PhD, Director, Beck Institute for Cognitive Therapy and Research, Clinical Associate Professor of Psychology in Psychiatry, University of Pennsylvania

"With understanding and kindness, Dr. Jeff helps parents acknowledge what we are all ashamed to admit: that sometimes our children drive us crazy, and we don't like them very much. Through his own experience as a parent and a licensed psychologist, Dr. Jeff skillfully guides parents to discover how toxic thoughts actually support our children's frustrating behavior! If you want to improve and deepen your relationship with your children, this book is a must-read!"
  —JEANNE ELIUM AND DON ELIUM, authors of *Raising a Son* and *Raising a Daughter*

"Jeffrey Bernstein has given us easy to absorb, insightful tips that will change the way we think about what our kids do, and why they do it. This book will not only make parenting more gratifying; it will help make life more gratifying."
  —MYRNA B. SHURE, PhD, author of *Raising a Thinking Child*

"The threshold between experiencing parental "love" and parental "like" can be a blurry one indeed, but both processes are essential to engage in if families are to develop in healthy and creative ways. In *Liking the Child You Love*, Dr. Jeffrey Bernstein gently but skillfully guides parents through the many emotional challenges of childrearing. Combining illuminating case examples with wise and practical strategies, *Liking the Child You Love* will be of inestimable value to mothers and fathers alike at every stage of family development."
  —DR. BRAD SACHS, author of *The Good Enough Child* and *The Good Enough Teen*

"I wholeheartedly recommend Dr. Jeff's book because his premise—that although we love our kids—sometimes it can be much harder to like them—is very important. It's often easier to love our children than to actually like them. The author helps parents keep their cool when their children are at their most challenging and paves the way for increased parental empathy."
  —NANCY SAMALIN, MS, author of *Loving Your Child is Not Enough* and *Love and Anger: The Parental Dilemma*

"No parent wants to be put over the edge by their child's negative behavior, and with Jeffrey Bernstein's *Liking the Child You Love,* you won't have to be. Bernstein provides parents with a creative and accessible roadmap out of the toxic reactions to their children's negative behavior, reactions which only trigger more undesirable behavior. Now parents can stop blaming themselves and their kids when

DISCARDED

things start to spiral, and instead know exactly what to do and say to be the loving and effective parents they want to be."
—TAMAR E. CHANSKY, PhD, author of *Freeing Your Child from Negative Thinking* and *Freeing Your Child from Anxiety*

"Dr. Bernstein addresses a huge missing piece of the parenting puzzle: How you feel about your kids is determined to a large extent by how you think—and a parent's thoughts can be pretty screwy sometimes! This book provides an excellent corrective for parents' emotional upsets and a straightforward path toward a happier family."
—THOMAS W. PHELAN, PhD, author of *1-2-3 Magic: Effective Discipline for Children 2-12*

"Bravo, Dr. Jeff, for helping parents admit that they don't always like their children. I highly recommend this book for all those parents who want to run away from home or hide in the bathroom until their child outgrows a difficult stage. This book has the cure for Parent Frustration Syndrome. It will help you identify and avoid self-sabotaging thoughts and behaviors that compromise your relationship with the child you deeply love."
—KAREN DEERWESTER, author of *The Entitlement-Free Child*

"Dr. Jeff recounts the joys and trials he has experienced with his own children. And this openness adds both credence and clarity to his enjoyable and thoughtful book. This is a delightful, check-yourself-out-while-you-learn experience that I recommend to all parents who might occasionally say to themselves, 'I'm not sure I like this child I love!'"
—FOSTER CLINE, MD, Founder and author of *Parenting with Love and Logic*

"Say 'Goodbye' to being at your wit's end with your child's behavior and feeling guilty about how you react. *Liking the Child You Love* helps you understand *your* frustrations and walks you through the emotional struggles of raising children. Say "Hello" to a stronger connection to your child *now,* not long after he's grown and out of the house."
—SUSAN NEWMAN, PhD, author of *Little Things Long Remembered: Making Your Children Feel Special Every Day*

"As a writer of literature for children and adolescents, I spend a great deal of time trying to get into their heads and hearts. I have had great success with the children I have interviewed over the years. It's my own brood that·has had me stumped.
    If truth be known, I couldn't put this book down. Within the first hour, I was taking notes. Liking the child you love is harder than one would think and often hard to admit. But I can't believe there is a parent anywhere who hasn't met this dichotomy firsthand. This is an enormously helpful book and easily digestible for those of us whose plates are already too full. I highly recommend this read to all parents and those who want to like the children they love."
—AUDREY PENN, author of *The Kissing Hand*

Liking
the Child
You Love

Build a Better Relationship
with Your Kids—Even When
They're Driving You Crazy

JEFFREY BERNSTEIN, PhD

Da Capo
LIFE
LONG

A Member of the Perseus Books Group

646.78
Pter

Many of the designations used by manufacturers and sellers to distinguish their products are claimed as trademarks. Where those designations appear in this book and Da Capo Press was aware of a trademark claim, the designations have been printed in initial capital letters.

Copyright © 2009 by Jeffrey Bernstein

All rights reserved. No part of this publication may be reproduced, stored in a retrieval system, or transmitted, in any form or by any means, electronic, mechanical, photocopying, recording, or otherwise, without the prior written permission of the publisher. Printed in the United States of America. For information, address Da Capo Press, 11 Cambridge Center, Cambridge, MA 02142.

Set in 11 point Fairfield LH Light by the Perseus Books Group

Library of Congress Cataloging-in-Publication Data

Bernstein, Jeffrey, 1961–
    Liking the child you love : build a better relationship with your kids—even when they're driving you crazy / Jeffrey Bernstein.
        p. cm.
    Includes bibliographical references and index.
    ISBN 978-0-7382-1261-6 (alk. paper)
    1. Parent and child. 2. Parenting. I. Title.
HQ755.85.B476 2009
646.7'8dc—22

                                                                        2009005717

First Da Capo Press edition 2009

Published by Da Capo Press
A Member of the Perseus Books Group
www.dacapopress.com

Note: The information in this book is true and complete to the best of our knowledge. This book is intended only as an informative guide for those wishing to know more about health issues. In no way is this book intended to replace, countermand, or conflict with the advice given to you by your own physician. The ultimate decision concerning care should be made between you and your doctor. We strongly recommend you follow his or her advice. Information in this book is general and is offered with no guarantees on the part of the author or Da Capo Press. The authors and publisher disclaim all liability in connection with the use of this book. The names and identifying details of people associated with events described in this book have been changed. Any similarity to actual persons is coincidental.

Da Capo Press books are available at special discounts for bulk purchases in the U.S. by corporations, institutions, and other organizations. For more information, please contact the Special Markets Department at the Perseus Books Group, 2300 Chestnut Street, Suite 200, Philadelphia, PA, 19103, or call (800) 810-4145, ext. 5000, or e-mail special.markets@perseusbooks.com.

10 9 8 7 6 5 4 3 2 1

Alissa, Sam, and Gabby you are amazing children and wonderful teachers. Loving all three of you has been effortless. And through it all, being your dad continues to be the biggest joy and highest honor of my life.

Contents

Author's Note

This book is intended to be educational in nature and is not intended as a substitute for professional help. Please bear in mind that the formal diagnosis and treatment of any mental health conditions, including any mentioned in this book, should be made by a qualified health care professional. Although I share many examples from my psychology practice in this book, all names and identifying information have been changed to protect client confidentiality.

The strategies I suggest are aimed at parents of all ages of children, through eighteen and even beyond. However, I use the term *child* to simplify the text rather than using terms such as *toddler*, *teenager*, or *young adult*. Please also note that, where possible, I alternate *he* and *she* between chapters to reflect my intention to balance gender representation.

How Can I Be a Good Parent and Have These Bad Thoughts?

Nothing impacts your child more than the way you, his parent, perceive him. As parents, we strive to like the child we love. What I mean by *like* is feeling positive about our children's thoughts, reactions, attitudes, and values. As parents, we "light up" about how wonderful it feels to like the way our child is behaving. It is when we don't like our child's attitude and behavior, however, that we lose that warm, fuzzy feeling and things don't feel so comfortable. Even though most parents really do love their children, they find it quite disturbing when they catch themselves thinking not-so-nice thoughts toward their kids.

Parenting can be highly challenging. I recall one day some years ago when my kids were giving me a hard time about cleaning their rooms. My immediate feeling was that by not doing what I asked—actually, what I demanded—they were being disrespectful. I was getting frustrated, to say the least. So in stepping back from the situation and believing I was "Father knows best" and also a well-adjusted psychologist, I called on my best coping skills—yep, I called up my mother and whined.

Having written books on parenting, you might think I'd easily be able to handle my own kids, right? Well, not that day. And, quite honestly, I have had my share of those days, just like you. As much as I love my kids, I have still struggled with angry thoughts about them that seem to come out of nowhere. Let's just say that being a parent has been, and continues to be, the most challenging job I have ever had. It is a true labor of love.

What were those thoughts whipping around in my mind that I shared with my mother? Perhaps you can relate:

"They don't appreciate anything I do for them."

"They are so *spoiled.*"

"They just suck me dry."

"Fine, I'll let them be lazy, and someday they'll learn their lesson."

"They say they hate me, and, well, I'm not so crazy about them either."

I have a few other gems I could share, but you get the idea. That day my mother listened, listened some more, and helped me calm down. After reflecting on my mom's ever-supportive voice of reason, I had a tremendous "Aha!" experience: Although most of us know when we are upset, we don't consciously focus on how much our own thoughts play a role in our emotional upheaval. ***Most parents overlook how much their thoughts about their children impact how they feel toward and react to them, for better or worse.***

Okay, you may be saying, "Hey, Dr. Jeff, no kidding! And, as a psychologist, *when* did you finally figure this out?" My response is that sometimes the most obvious and simple truths are the most elusive. That day it really hit me just how powerful and influential those thoughts can be. I could now clearly see how I was wreaking havoc on my own ability to accurately understand my children's needs.

Having worked with more than two thousand parents and children as clients and workshop participants in twenty years, I have personally seen over and over again parents mired in toxic thinking. Given the pace of modern life and all the stresses we face, this problem can only be getting worse. As I thought more about it, I realized how widespread and insidious it is.

Dana, for example, an exasperated mother in my practice, one day exemplified the frustration of so many parents I see. "Dr. Jeff, I feel so guilty saying this, but I just feel many days that I don't like my impossible, bratty eleven-year-old daughter anymore. I don't understand why it has gotten to this point." Dana's eyes filled with tears.

Another client of mine, Julian, father of three teenagers *and* a newborn, reflected Dana's concerns in a more humorous way. He said, "Jeff, now I know why some animals eat their young."

As parents, we want our children to feel loved, understood, accepted, and appreciated. To make this happen, we give to our children emotionally, spiritually, physically, materially, and in any other realm we can think of. Yet many parents find themselves steaming with frustration when they give all they can to their children. This is because it's so easy to think ourselves into misery when hammered with challenging, difficult, and even defiant behaviors from our kids. These thoughts are common and normal. ***But getting a handle on parental toxic thinking can actually improve your children's defiant behavior and give you a happier family relationship.***

If you're reading this book, I assume you too feel like one of these parents, at least from time to time. Maybe you wish you could wave a magical "contentment wand," and finally your child would be easier to deal with! The reality is that parenting is very challenging.

Here's the good news—you are not alone. In fact, it may blow your mind how much company you have. Parents everywhere—whether married, remarried, single, widowed, young, or old—right at this moment, are fed up. Go to a supermarket, hang out at an amusement park, or even perk up your ears in a restaurant, and you will see and hear parents having problems in paradise. They are unhappy and disgusted and are tired of or plain worn out from what I term Parent Frustration Syndrome (PFS). I describe PFS more fully in Chapter 1.

Why Is Parenting So Hard?

From the time our kids are little, we parents have to think of the big picture. We choose the best opportunities we can for our kids, and we hope that they will choose the best things for themselves as they get older. Ironically, perhaps the biggest challenge to our success as parents is our anxiety that our children will not be happy and content.

As we raise our children, we also raise the bar for their success over our own. On our deathbeds, we'll want to know we did right by our children. And most kids know their parents want the best for them. At the same time, when kids make mistakes or encounter disappointments, parents suffer through them too. This fuels the anxiety we have as parents.

It is largely this anxiety that keeps burning toxic thoughts into our brains. When we worry about our children, we tend to think *negatively* and *dramatically*—we naturally assume the worst. This leads to more troubled feelings: more anxiety mixed with anger, sadness, resignation, and frustration. Some parents silently stew, and others "lose it" by overreacting to their children, and then many feel tremendous guilt. To be sure, not too many kids come into my office feeling good about unspoken tensions or being yelled at.

Parents often vow to "cool it" and be more understanding and patient with their children. Too often, however, they are besieged by toxic thoughts and fall back into the overwhelming forces of PFS. Without the tools to change your tune, you will keep singing the same parenting song.

Parents' Perceptions Influence Children's Realities

Parents typically seek me out for help when children have problems such as verbal or physical outbursts, anxiety or depression, legal concerns, drug-related issues, problems with peers and family, and school difficulties. Often, when I meet with kids and their parents, the emotional tensions are off the chart.

I love working with kids who are struggling because as they learn more effective ways to cope and deal with life, I feel very satisfied. Yet working with kids usually means working with their parents, too—and they are often not very happy when their children are driving them crazy. The longer I practice as a psychologist, the more I see the powerful influence that parents play in shaping their children's lives. Together, we can guide their children to make healthy changes in the way they cope with the challenges they face.

Despite my experience and attempts to be supportive, I still have to make sure that I proceed with caution when helping parents see their role in their children's issues. I am not in any way blaming the parents for their children's problems. At the same time, it is enlightening for parents to learn how their own thinking patterns contribute to the problems they experience with their children. Simply put, how you think about your child impacts how you like your child and how your child likes himself. Your perceptions also influence how your child copes with problems. We all know adults who report the value of having parents who believed in them while growing up.

It Really Is About You

Because the examples in this book are, for the most part, parent-thought centered, it may seem like I am holding parents overly responsible for their children's behavior. However, when you temporarily put aside what your child is doing and devote yourself to changing your own thoughts and actions, it can have a tremendously positive effect on your *child's* behavior.

You will learn in this book that you—much more than your child—are the source of your PFS. It is your thoughts about what your kids do or don't do that drive you crazy. Once you learn to get control of your thoughts, then you will also get control of your emotions and reactions. And, most important, you and your child will have a closer, more understanding relationship.

My first book, *Why Can't You Read My Mind?* addressed the toxic-thinking problem in intimate relationships. Since that time, I have written two books on parenting, *10 Days to a Less Defiant Child* and *10 Days to a Less Distracted Child*. I am humbled by and grateful for the letters and e-mails from readers around the world who have praised my books. At the same time, I felt a need now to go boldly where most parenting self-help books do not: into the dark thoughts of anxious, frustrated parents.

Parents thinking toxically about their own kids is a huge, unexamined, and underrecognized problem. Yet it is so important to solve because, left unchecked, it creates negative emotions and behaviors. These negative feelings have an enormous impact on the happiness of your family. This book will help you overcome your negative thoughts so that you can be more clearheaded in parenting your children. I have packed this book with the same strategies that I offer to parents in my practice.

When parents first bring their child to see me, I encourage them to share their child's positive qualities—right in front of the very child they love so much but may, at the time, like so little. These parents are suffering from major PFS, and the child is hurting from the repercussions. By beginning with the child's strengths in mind, I am infusing hope and positive energy from day one. I am also showing the parent and child how powerful perceptions can be. Once they feel safe and share their frustrations, parents also learn how underlying toxic thoughts, if not zapped, can swallow up these positive intentions and connections.

Whether your child is occasionally difficult or often defiant, the tools in this book will be highly beneficial for you, your child, and your relationship with him. As you gain control over your toxic thoughts and speak and behave less reactively to your child, he will likely follow your lead and think and act less disruptively, too. As you will see, toxic thoughts are rigid, unfair, and distorted perceptions—for example, "She never applies herself in anything she does." Although you may feel that the problems rest with your child and you're not the one who needs to change, please keep an open mind. The more you get free of toxic thoughts and try in earnest to gain from the insights that this book offers, the more your kids will change for the better as well.

My Past Pattern of Overreacting and Misunderstanding

I used to be an overreactive and irritated parent. Getting rid of my toxic thoughts got rid of my PFS—big time. Make no mistake, I still have to work on controlling my thoughts. But once I learned how to do it, I came a long way in a short time. And getting control over my toxic thoughts cleared the way to understanding my children better than I ever could have imagined.

I have worked on understanding myself and my children more than I have worked on anything else in my life. And the more that I understand them, the more joy I get from them and they get from me. The most wonderful gift I have given myself is being more patient, more understanding, and less reactive toward my kids. I have learned how to put things in a healthy perspective. No more do my toxic thoughts so powerfully warp and distort my mind and thwart my ability to connect with and enjoy my kids. I am thrilled at how much more I have learned to appreciate the children whom I love so much.

How to Use This Book

Chapters 1–3 lay the groundwork for understanding what toxic thoughts are and how to become mindful of them. Chapters 4–7 are more strategic and offer tools involving relaxation, mindfulness, and alternative thoughts. You will learn how to counter slower-burning toxic thoughts as well as those that tend to flare up more rapidly. You'll learn how to overcome the nine toxic-thought patterns that plague families:

1. The "always or never" trap
2. Label gluing
3. Seething sarcasm
4. Smoldering suspicions
5. Detrimental denial
6. Emotional overheating
7. Blame blasting
8. "Should" slamming
9. Dooming conclusions

The remaining chapters provide knowledge and strategies for discipline, using positive reinforcement, and enjoying life as a parent. I encourage you to keep a journal of your thoughts and feelings from this point on. The more that you capture what goes on in your head and employ the strategies provided in this book, the more active and successful you will be in creating positive changes. There are exercises in different chapters and space to write in your thoughts and reflections. You can easily copy these formats in your journal. Anything you respond to in these pages or think up on your own can be included. Feel free to use whatever format for recording thoughts and feelings that works best for you.

I am excited for you to learn how to detoxify your mind. My clients who put these principles in place with their children have told me that *all* relationships in their lives improve once they are free from the shackles of toxic thinking. They find that they feel better not only toward their children but also toward spouses and intimate partners (for more on this, read *Why Can't You Read My Mind?*), co-workers, friends, and extended family. Why? Because people who suffer from toxic thinking often don't have problems only in their parenting but tend to have problems in their other relationships as well.

Keep the Faith as You Go Forward

I hope that if you have plans for a one-way plane ticket for peeved parents, you won't board just yet—at least not until you read this book. Please seize this opportunity for joy and connection with your child. With due humility, I have personally helped more than two thousand parents and kids have more harmonious, joyous relationships with this advice and information.

Yes, now you can like the child you love in ways you never imagined. You don't have to wait until he is twenty-five or even thirty-five to finally enjoy each other and for him to appreciate all your sacrifice and work. Trust me, as you change for the better by getting free of your toxic thoughts, he will have a better attitude, too.

No longer will you fall prey to emotional hijackings where you lose it "all of a sudden." You will learn what your toxic thoughts are and how to stop them from overtaking you. And, most important, you will learn how to like the child you love much more.

Chapter 1

Why Liking Your Child Is Much Harder than Loving Him

B EING A PARENT can be very emotionally rewarding, but it can also be draining and frustrating. And when your child gets to you, I know how very upsetting it can be. You may even feel like you are at your wit's end. But hang on—help is on the way in the pages that follow.

Susan, the mother of an eleven-year-old boy, was highly distraught when she came in to see me. Visibly shaken and in the throes of Parent Frustration Syndrome, she said, "Dr. Jeff, it is just one thing after another with Tommy. I've had it up to here," motioning to her throat. She continued, "Today, nonstop, he kept taunting me, and then when I got mad, he called me a 'crappy mother.' On top of all this, he always picks on his younger brother." She then echoed the sentiment of so many parents I listen to: "I do so much for him, and he's the one treating *me* like crap. And if I talked *that way* to *my* parents, I would have been smacked right across the face. You know what? That's what I feel like doing. He's just a spoiled brat who never realizes how good he has it!"

Susan then finished her volley of frustration by serving up the grand slam: "Dr. Jeff, sometimes I can't stand Tommy, and I feel horrible saying this about my own son. But he gets under my skin and makes me want to pull my hair out! I am so exhausted from

1

him. I swear, I feel like I don't even like him anymore. Am I crazy for feeling this way?"

I assured Susan that she was not crazy. I helped her work through her negative thoughts and feelings toward Tommy, and she learned to control her reactions. Most important, as you too will learn, Susan was soon able not to let her dislike for her son's attitude and behaviors get in the way of understanding what was troubling him. She also discovered how she could choose not to get herself worked up into an emotional frenzy when Tommy was difficult. This breakthrough was very liberating to Susan. The great news is that this book will help you get to this better parenting place as well.

To the best of my knowledge, you will not find the term *Parent Frustration Syndrome* in any medical or psychology textbook. But it describes a very real problem that millions of mothers and fathers face every day. PFS results when a parent feels emotionally overwhelmed and discouraged about her parenting efforts and her child's attitude and behaviors. Parents struggling with PFS may feel any one or more of the following:

- moderately to highly frustrated
- resentful of their children's misbehaviors, their lack of expressed gratitude, and possibly even their struggles
- moderately to significantly sad or even depressed
- pessimistic in their outlook of their children's lives
- desiring to escape family pressures
- questioning their own value
- a sense of inadequacy in thinking their children's struggles compare worse to those of extended family and friends
- confused about why their children act in ways that don't make sense
- less joy
- disheartened and guilty that family life is less gratifying than hoped for

The good news is that I am very confident that PFS can be greatly managed, if not cured, by using in earnest the strategies in this book.

Let's see how you register on the PFS meter. If you have felt or feel any of the following, then you have PFS, at least to some degree.

How Much Do You Suffer from PFS?

It can be helpful for you to get a handle on how you feel when your child is driving you up the wall. Most frustrated parents can identify with at least a few of the following at one time or another. Feel free to check off those that you can relate to:

You resent how your difficult child has drained you
    and the rest of the family.   _____

You feel desperately overwhelmed trying to keep up
    with all of life's demands.   _____

You feel nothing is going to help your situation.   _____

You can't understand why your child acts better
    behaved around other adults than with you.   _____

You feel exhausted.   _____

You can't comprehend why your child acts this way,
    especially since you try so hard to be a good parent.   _____

You feel manipulated.   _____

You question why you had children in the first place.   _____

You feel sad that your marriage has lost its passion.   _____

You are easily angered yet feel guilty for being so
    frustrated.   _____

As a single parent, you feel it is impossible to stay sane.   _____

You feel like a horrible failure as a parent.   _____

This list of PFS-related thoughts is representative but certainly not exhaustive. Parents who get frustrated start to feel much better when they gain control over what is going on in their heads. This is because it is very hard to gain control of your child, your own feelings, or anything else in your life until you first gain control of your thoughts.

In reading this book, you will learn how to detoxify your thoughts and will experience wonderful changes in your relationship with your child. You will no longer feel burned out, and you will avoid fruitless power struggles.

One day when writing this chapter, I had to deal with an acute flare-up of my own PFS. My three children were having a blast decorating holiday gingerbread cookies, and of course, my kitchen consequently looked like a condemned living area. Thinking back to years gone by when I used to "lose it" with my kids, I found myself swelling with pride. After all, my kids were having fun, even though they were messing up the kitchen. "No big deal, and besides, what a fantastic dad I am," I thought.

Just as I scanned the area, noting how we would all eventually clean up the mess, a large bottle of sprinkles was knocked off the counter and spilled all over the floor. Immediately, I felt my blood pressure rise. I then heard myself saying in a strained voice, "How can I love you so much when I feel at the same time like I want to explode?" My son then quipped, "Dad, isn't that why you are writing that new book about problems liking your kids?"

My son was right. I am writing this book to help parents like you. This book is about setting you free to look at what so many parents feel guilty talking about: your negative thoughts and feelings toward your own children. There—ugh—I said it. Now you can take a deep breath and keep reading.

I know how alone you have been feeling. You wonder, "Why is it that parents don't *really* talk about their dark thoughts and frustrations and what they don't like about their children?" You may even ask, "Is it that *their* children are *not* challenging and my child *is*?" Let me reassure you that this is definitely not so. Nearly all parents feel this way, and I will help you discover what fuels your emotional struggles with your child. And better yet, I'm going to show you what you can do about it. Just hang with me—you'll see soon enough.

Parenting Is Hard Work, but It's a Job You Can't Quit

Parenting is difficult—that's for sure. The mere concept of caring for and raising a child in today's anxiety-laden, competitive world is daunting and overwhelming. Although the following may not hit an all-time high on the profundity scale, I'm going to say it anyway: Once you have kids, there is no longer the option to stop being a parent. Most parents begin the child-rearing journey with expectations of jubilance and boundless joy. The wonderful news is that you certainly do get a lot of that by being a parent. Yet in contrast, you may also be shocked at some of the challenging and even harrowing realities that arise when you face problems and conflicts with your kids. Add to this stress the realities of trying to work, be married, and balance it all, and you end up with PFS. You realize that you love your kids, but it certainly is not always a joyous experience.

Take a look at a humorous bulletin on the following page about a "job description" that a client forwarded to me.

PARENT WANTED
POSITION :

Mom, Mommy, Mama, Ma
Dad, Daddy, Dada, Pa, Pop

JOB DESCRIPTION:

Long-term team players needed for challenging, permanent work in an often chaotic environment.

Candidates must possess excellent communication and organizational skills and be willing to work variable hours, which will include evenings and weekends and frequent twenty-four-hour shifts on call.

Some overnight travel required; travel expenses not reimbursed.

Extensive courier duties also required.

RESPONSIBILITIES:

The rest of your life.

Must be willing to be hated, at least temporarily, until someone needs five dollars.

Must be willing to bite tongue repeatedly.

Also, must possess the physical stamina of a pack mule.

Must screen phone calls, maintain calendars, and coordinate production of multiple homework projects.

Must have ability to plan and organize social gatherings for clients of all ages and mental outlooks.

Must be willing to be indispensable one minute, an embarrassment the next.

Must always hope for the best but be prepared for the worst.

Must assume final, complete accountability for the quality of the end product.

Responsibilities also include floor maintenance and janitorial work throughout the facility.

I find this parent job description to be quite funny. I hope you do, too. The reality is that the more that we, as parents, can call upon such humor, the easier it is to deal with the pressures that do come with the job. And no joke—it is a job!

On a more serious note, humor and other calming forces are often not in parents' minds when they need them most. Instead, most parents are flooding themselves with negativity. Regretfully, sometimes what is in our heads explodes out of our mouths.

Dealing with Difficult Feelings Is Not Easy

Since you are reading this book, I would guess that you are a parent suffering through some PFS. I am here to tell you that if you feel you don't like some of your child's attitudes and behaviors, that is okay. Or if, for example, you "can't stand" those behaviors, then that is fine too—as long as you deal with these thoughts and feelings. Actually, it is your love for your child that makes it even more maddening when you find yourself flooded with negative feelings. Even if you don't like your child as a person right now, as long as you do something constructive with these negative feelings, that is perfectly acceptable.

I find it rewarding to help you explore and overcome your parenting struggles. Facing my own challenges and pitfalls as a father and growing from them has been the most satisfying part of my life. I am pleased that you are letting me guide you to a better place.

I know it can be uncomfortable to explore your struggles. Self-awareness can feel threatening and scary because it requires you to move out of your comfort zone. Yes, challenging your negative thoughts and feelings is unfamiliar and unpleasant. Yet I can also say with unswerving conviction that the rewards of better understanding your negative feelings toward your children, and doing something positive about them, are invaluable.

I am here to create the safety that you need to explore the dark side of your parenting mind. I also am here to empower you to work through your negative feelings. Parents may joke on soccer game sidelines, in supermarkets, at parties, or in other social settings about how they struggle with their children's behaviors. Yet these amusing "my kid is driving me crazy" anecdotes usually only scratch the surface of what these parents actually struggle with. You know this by just how upset you get with your own children and how overwhelming it can be. I am here to help you understand these emotional struggles. This is very important for your sanity, but also in understanding your child.

Your Mind Is the Culprit

The most exciting thing you will learn in this book is how your own mind creates far more negative feelings toward your children than your kids themselves do. That's right—it really all begins and ends with what you say to yourself about your kids. In the words of noted author Anaïs Nin, "We don't see things as they are; we see things as we are."

As I mentioned earlier, anxiety is prevalent for parents because we are responsible for the safety and well-being of our kids. Our desire for our children to "turn out well" also stimulates worry and angst. Toxic thoughts are formed and fueled when we feel our children are not doing what they need to do or are making poor choices. As you will see, in addition to our anxiety, how we perceive our children and our role as parents can also be a springboard to toxic thinking.

Do you hold negative perceptions and even perhaps prejudices toward your own children? I'm not positive what your answer is, but my sense is that if you really look inward, you'll say yes. What I *am* positive about is that these negative views and related feelings can compromise your parenting efforts and connection with your child.

Think about it: Prejudice is a "prejudgment," a snap decision about your child before you know (or allow yourself to know) the realities about him or the circumstances he faces. Growing up, you absorbed some beliefs about how you would raise children. In the process, you wittingly and unwittingly got on board with certain biases or prejudices. Some of our parenting prejudices are hundreds or even thousands of years old.

For example, we have all heard "Spare the rod and spoil the child." This saying promotes the idea that children will flourish only if punished, physically or otherwise, for any wrongdoing. Parents following this line of thinking tend to be rigid in expectations and highly reactive. Most people in this era challenge the view of physical punishment as a form of discipline. Even so, minus the hitting, the rigid "I am in charge of you" mentality can get in the way of fostering cooperation with your child and backfire.

Another negative view is the aphorism "Children should be seen and not heard." It suggests that children's opinions don't count or are not credible. Although few people have such a denigrating notion of children, this belief, or at least diluted forms of it, persists in common usage.

There is also another negative view of children that one might think is more recent, though it really isn't: "The younger generation is spoiled and entitled." The following quote speaks to this view: "The children now love luxury; they have bad manners, contempt for authority; they show disrespect for elders and love chatter in place of exercise. Children are now tyrants, not the servants of their households. They no longer rise when elders enter the room. They contradict their parents, chatter before company, gobble up dainties at the table, cross their legs, and tyrannize their teachers." Surprise, surprise—these were the words of Socrates from only around two thousand years ago. Talk about all of us parents living in a time warp!

Most parents try to view their children in a more positive light than these broad biases may suggest. Granted, this may be easier for parents *before* their children learn to speak. At the same time, these "pearls of wisdom" represent an underlying view that children do not have equal rights to adults. Don't our children deserve the same right to be understood that we as adults value?

By the way, overly idealistic visions of children and family life can be just as problematic. Some parents hold themselves to unrealistic expectations of perfection. We are inculcated with Hallmark card–like images of beaming parents at soccer games, school events, graduations, and marriage ceremonies, yet the reality is that family life has ups and downs.

Please don't think I am a cynic. I am concerned, however, that some parents are not prepared as much for the lows as they are for the highs. Let's take a closer look at how your views inform how you handle the lows.

Family-of-Origin Experiences Affect Parents, Too

One day, in a shopping center parking lot, I overheard a young father shout at his young daughter, "How many times do I gotta tell you!" I then heard her start to cry. I thought, "I wonder where he learned to speak in such a shaming tone to his daughter? Perhaps he heard that from his own parents."

I certainly see many parents who speak to their children in negative and shaming ways. I have been guilty of it myself in the past and try to be vigilant to no longer speak in this manner. Even if occasionally they contain hints of truth, these types of phrases are very painful to children. They include:

"Can't you ever think for yourself?"

"You are lazy."

"Don't you ever think about anything?"

"Why can't you be more like _____ [your sister, brother, cousin, friend]?"

"It's all your fault."

"You just don't appreciate anything."

"You never listen."

"See—you always have to learn the hard way."

I think you probably get the picture. As you will soon see, these toxic words come from toxic thinking. Parents, in many cases, pass on destructive ways of thinking and talking from one generation to another. Children on the receiving end of such verbalizations, however, don't know why their parents say such things and can feel deeply hurt and resentful.

Each Parent Will Have Personal Child-Rearing Opinions

I am not here to tell you what to believe in or not to believe in. I am hoping, however, that you are willing to become more aware of what is working and not working in your relationship with your child. Any limiting beliefs, biases, and prejudices you may hold are worth exploring. Look at which thoughts get you mired in negative energy regarding your child's attitudes and behaviors.

One area where strong personal views are common is discipline and punishment, especially among what I call "consequence-ravenous" parents; they are foaming at the mouth and starving to dole out justice for bad behavior. In my previous book *10 Days to a Less Defiant Child*, I included a chapter titled "Dependable Discipline," in which I explained how, for defiant children, consequences can often backfire and fuel further defiant behavior. This is because with defiant children, bypassing their emotional reactivity works *better* than inflaming it. Please understand that I am not against consequences for kids. I am concerned, however, that when consequences are imposed in a rigid, harsh, and overboard manner, challenging children and teens will likely rebel even more. The more there is a strong, positive connection between parent and child, the fewer consequences will be needed. When consequences are effective, they are best delivered in a collaborative, not adversarial, manner. I will talk more about discipline and consequences in Chapter 8.

Societal and historical forces, one's family of origin, and personal views are not the only sources that form and maintain parents' beliefs about how to raise children. Cultural and generational influences as well as what is conveyed in the media all serve to shape what we think parenting is or is not. As you read, I am asking you to keep an open mind about your own beliefs and how they work for you or against you as you raise your child.

The Stakes Are High

It is obvious that the quality of the parent-child relationship bears a heavy influence on children as they grow into adulthood. Unfortunately, many parents don't adequately deal with their negative feelings toward their very own children. Parents who cannot cope with their challenging children and teens can act unfairly or lash out at their kids, deepening mutual hurts, creating lingering tensions, and fueling more problematic behaviors in kids, often with tragic results.

Let's be clear that kids, especially challenging ones, don't always make it easy on parents. I recall, for example, a girl who admitted to me that she wanted to fail eighth grade to "piss off my parents even more." Yet children of fractured parenting relationships often go on to lead fractured lives. Deep down they feel hurt and wish they could have more connection with their parent(s). Of course, this correlation is not absolute. Some kids find other supportive adults such as other family members or teachers to guide them. And some kids may be more naturally resilient than others. Nonetheless, kids who have positive relationships with their parents will likely have some major advantages in facing life's demands.

I have seen many adults in my psychology practice suffering from deep emotional scars because they perceived that their own parents did not like them enough or, even worse, love them in a healthy way. Most disconcerting is that many adults who end up holding on to their own parents' disapproval and dislike end up confusing this as feeling not loved. For many, it takes years to work through the resultant damage. Unfortunately, for some, it gnaws away at their ability to experience joy throughout their lives. The bottom line is that the quality of the parent-child relationship is crucial to raising an emotionally healthy adult.

The sad truth is that disliking your child's behaviors or even him as a whole is a feeling that won't go away unless you deal with it. For example, consider seventy-year-old Alice, who was working through feelings of dislike toward her forty-year-old daughter. The embedded conflicts were in essence the same as thirty years earlier when the mother was forty and the daughter was ten. Neither one felt understood by the other. In this family, Alice was upset that her daughter Claudia felt that Alice still favored her two older sisters. Although this very same basic mother-child conflict had existed for many years, the content of the issues changed over time. In the counseling process, both mother and daughter learned to understand one another and, in turn, to like one another a whole lot more.

When I struggled with my own PFS, the most humbling reality was discovering that my negative reactions were due to my own immaturity and *not* my children's. To be sure, I am not now a perfect dad, nor are my kids perfect. But I now am perfectly aware that unless I truly understand the sources of my children's frustrations, then I cannot control my own when dealing with them. And, to best understand my children's frustrations, I first have to understand my own. The reality is that I still have to work on being an effective parent every day.

We all make mistakes. I often say to my clients, "The only perfect people are in the cemetery." As parents, we can all feel proud of the times we handle our frustrations well with our kids. We can also have those not-so-good days where we may feel we don't like things about our children. The important thing is getting yourself back up when you fall down and doing the right thing for yourself and for your child. Getting control over your toxic thoughts will take you far in having more good days than bad ones.

A wise colleague of mine once pointed out to me that it is when kids are most unlovable that we must love them the most. I would also say it is just as important that when kids are most *unlikable* we must *understand* them the most. The rest of this chapter is devoted to introducing what is involved in understanding and liking your child.

You Can't Hide Dislike from Your Child

It is hard to conceal your dislike of your child's negative behaviors. As a psychologist, I often see parents who think they can cloak their negative feelings and keep them under the radar. They think that if they can ignore these thoughts, they will go away. Too often, though, these feelings are detected by the child or teen, damaging their self-esteem, as children often share with me with tears streaming down their faces. The reality is that children pick up on parents' negative thoughts and feelings *more* than parents realize.

Dislike Makes Understanding Disappear

Your feelings of dislike undermine your ability to understand your child, and the most powerful gift you can give to your child is to understand him. Parents' dislikes are important to take seriously and overcome because they can create misunderstandings, and misunderstandings lead to more dislike. Dislikes and misunderstandings shatter bonds of trust between parents and children, even when there is love.

The bottom line is this: Liking is the missing link for understanding your child. Ironically, most parents think, "I don't like you right now, so why should I *even try* to understand you?" This line of reasoning is immature. The more you become skilled at dealing with your own toxic thoughts when your child acts difficult or is difficult for you to understand, the less frustrated you will be. You will not let him cause you to unravel and will be less likely to carry on like a child yourself.

Parents who can't turn the corner on their feelings of dislike grow increasingly distant from their children. I see this often in my practice. I am here to give you the tools to improve your ability to understand and enjoy your child.

In a very moving lecture that became a highly popular book, *The Last Lecture*, a Carnegie Mellon professor, Randy Paucsh, dying from cancer, quoted a respected colleague who said that usually if you don't like someone, it is because you have not spent enough time with him. However, in the case of our own children, I believe that if we feel we don't like them, it is because we have not opened ourselves up to accept them for who they are. Many parents spend much time with their children without being on the same wavelength as them. Getting at the root of your toxic thoughts will help you open up and tune in to your child's emotional frequency. Sadly, too many families go through the motions of coexistence without having the meaningful emotional connections that heal and protect from life's challenges and adversities.

Years ago, I saw a very angry and confused boy whose father was a "man's man" kind of guy. The father was an accomplished attorney and really into hunting and fishing. The son had an interest in fashion design, which his father had a hard time understanding and accepting. Years later, once the child had left the house, this father sat crying in my office, sharing how sad he was that his dislike for his son's interests, and fear that his son was gay, got in the way of their relationship. The father had difficulty understanding his son. Fortunately, the young man was willing to come in, and father and son finally connected with each other. It was heartwarming to see them put their judgments aside and really get to know each other.

I hope you and your child are connected. But despite whatever strain there may be in your relationship, this book will help you understand each other better, and restore and enhance your emotional connection.

Love Is Not Enough

Unconditional love can help us to be more understanding parents, but it is not enough. Many parents love their children, but they still don't really understand them. So what *does* get in the way of understanding your child? What gets in the way of enjoying your child? Why is it that your relationship with your child seems so up and down? My answer, as you likely know by now, to these questions is that it is your feelings of "like" (actually dislike) and not your feelings of love.

When you like your child, you want to spend time with her. You feel calm and patient around her. Perhaps the most important and healthy part of liking your child is remembering to see her world through her eyes and not just your own. What you see as clingy may be her need to connect. Her disrespectful comments that don't leave you feeling good, though not appropriate, may actually be her way of telling you that she is not feeling so good about herself. And her refusal to try may be in response to her feeling blocked by fear of failure. As you will see in this book, the more you can keep negative thoughts from blinding you toward your child's positive intentions, the better off you will both be. I believe that the importance of "like" in all relationships is, unfortunately, not given as much attention as love. And in some situations, it may even be more difficult to maintain than love. If you think about it, you may know of divorced couples who could, and even may still, love one another more easily than like each other.

Getting back to parenting, please complete the exercises below to examine your own thoughts about your child.

Exercise 1: Your Thoughts

What does loving your child mean to you?

_____

_____

_____

What does liking your child mean to you?

_____

_____

_____

What does not liking your child mean to you?

_____

_____

_____

• •

Which part of the exercise did you feel a stronger reaction to? Which did you have a fuller response to? My guess is that it was the love part. Love is the ideal we all fantasize about. Somewhere in the recesses of our brains we have been programmed to believe that we *should* unconditionally love our children. Striving for unconditional love is automatic for most parents. Although not all parents achieve it, overall I believe that most parents do a good job of loving their children. But many find that liking them is, by far, not as easy.

A Closer Look at the "Should" Problem

Please be reassured that you can be a wonderful, loving parent and still not like some characteristics and habits of your child. If these negative thoughts and consequent feelings are dealt with, then new understandings and closer connections can be established. What is problematic, however, is that many parents feel they *shouldn't* have feelings of dislike for their own children in the first place. By placing this pressure on themselves, parents end up even more frustrated—and feeling far more guilty than they need to. Some parents may also believe that they shouldn't have to work on managing their thoughts and feelings toward their children. These parents feel that unconditional love should mean unconditional like. Unfortunately, our minds don't necessarily work like that.

Noted psychologist Albert Ellis said, "Most people are like seagulls, they go around SHOULDING all over the place. They hold on to crazy ideas about the world and mess themselves and others up. They say stupid things like, 'He SHOULD do that!' or 'She SHOULDN'T do that!' or 'That SHOULDN'T happen!' But why should he do that? And why shouldn't she do that? And why shouldn't that happen?"

When it comes to life in general or parenting specifically, there are no universal laws. Saying that there should be less traffic on the way to work or that parenting shouldn't be so hard doesn't change anything. Yet even though these laws don't exist, we make ourselves upset when we feel they should. You don't have to like the things that your child does at times, but to say that they should not happen is just going to give you big-time PFS!

So keep in mind that *should* is a very tricky word. I tell all my clients that if they eliminate at least 75 percent of their use of the word *should*, they will feel better. No client has yet argued with me on this point. Nor *should* they! I will talk more about *should*s in Chapter 3 when I discuss "'should' slamming" as a toxic thinking pattern.

A Parent's Dislike Is Emotional Dynamite

You as a parent have an incredible impact, for better or worse, on how your child will feel about himself. Years and years of psychological research coupled with common sense shows this is crystal clear. You are committed to your child the rest of your life, and you can't divorce your child.

Although many parents beam with joy when their children are doing well, many also feel helpless, frustrated, and even resentful when their children are struggling or challenging. I have heard parents say to their kids, almost with pride, "I love you, but that does not mean I have to like what you are doing." Often, however, what children who hear this type of remark feel is "Oh, so you just don't like ME." And when kids sense dislike from their parents, they may disconnect from them.

Listening in on the Voice You Listened To

Over the years I have been honored to speak in front of many audiences. I have often had participants do the following exercise, which many found illuminating. The object is to get in touch with your parent's or (parents') voice of like, or dislike.

Exercise 2: Your Parent's Voice

Please sit down somewhere comfortable and dim the lights. Close your eyes and listen for your parent's voice. To get in the right frame of mind, think of the surroundings of your childhood. This means the sights, sounds, and smells. You may think of one or both parents. If you were raised by someone other than a parent, reflect on that person's voice. Just listen for a few minutes, and then open your eyes and write down what you heard.

_____

_____

_____

_____

_____

I hope this exercise evoked some pleasant memories for you. And, if not, rest assured that you are not alone. When I have done this exercise in groups, I have often seen adults who were misty-eyed with joy. I have also seen many who were teary-eyed with negative feelings about what their own parents said or thought about them. In considering your experience, ask yourself, "What voice and what words do I want my kids to remember me by?" They will hear and remember, for better or worse, much more than you realize.

Children Are Not the Only Casualties of Dislike

You know you love your child, and I know you do too—but you also know it is not always that simple. You feel lousy and guilty when you think unflattering thoughts about your kid. You then wonder, "Do other parents handle their kids more effectively than I do?" Have you ever wanted to give up? Or thought, "Maybe I am just not cut out to be a parent because it *should* be a lot easier than this"? Well, should it? I bet thinking this way drives you crazy.

Your Mind, for Better or Worse, Drives the Car

Keep in mind that this is a book for frustrated parents at all levels, not just those with high scores on the PFS meter. That's because all parents can gain immense benefits from learning how to like their children even when they are being obnoxious.

Although my message will be lighthearted in places, what I am sharing with you carries a lot of weight. I have spent more than twenty years listening to frustrated, fed-up children and frustrated, exasperated parents. I have often seen children and teens rocked by their parents' negative reactions, and in some cases it has led to very distressing situations.

How your child acts does not have to drive how you think about or react to him. You can break free of the shackles of guilt and learn once and for all how to help your child get ahead, and not lose your own head in the process. But you first must stop passively fantasizing that your child is going to wake up one day and spontaneously reform. Get real and lose that dream. And while you are at it, stop silently comparing your child to your neighbors' or relatives' children. We are in a very competitive world, and not every child will excel. Most children and teens are not on a mission to give their parents a hard time. But the reality is that life's challenges can wear out kids as well as parents. Pressure for grades, from peers, and to please their parents can be highly overwhelming for children. And who bears the brunt of their frustrations? You guessed it: their parents. That's what can wear you out—if you let it.

Before you slam this book down and say, "But Dr. Jeff, you don't understand—my kid *really* drives me nuts!" let me highlight that you are not alone in feeling this way. Take a look at the top-ten problem behaviors of children and teens faced by parents just like you. Although there is some levity to my list, trust me when I say that parents who react to these issues are often close to tears.

Dr. Jeff's Top-Ten List of What Parents Don't Like About Their Children

1. Leaving the house a mess
2. Erratic "deafness" about chores and schoolwork issues
3. Missing the school bus
4. Avoiding doing homework or forgetting to turn it in
5. Twisting what you say until you get confused
6. Shirking responsibility
7. Disrespectful attitude
8. Poor hygiene
9. Rude comments
10. Negative treatment of siblings

Now please fill in the blanks below for anything specific to
your kids that is not included in the above list:

_____

_____

_____

_____

• •

Such situations are not easy for any parent. However, neither do
they have to be *so hard*. The choice is in your hands. Think about
it: Why do the same stressors impact parents in very different
ways? As I will discuss further in Chapter 2, parents become overwhelmed with toxic thoughts such as "never," "always," "shouldn't,"
and other dooming perceptions about their children (for example,
"He's lazy and will be unproductive in society" or "He never appreciates all I sacrifice for him" or even "Go ahead and ruin your
life and see if I care"). The irony is that both you and your child
know you really do care. Consequently, and understandably, these
thoughts leave parents feeling discouraged and burned out. They
can't maintain positive feelings toward their children. The secret
to finally ridding yourself of the frustration, anger, disappointment,
and resentments that drive you to the breaking point is buried
within you. Don't panic—I am going to give you the tools to tackle
these toxic thoughts.

To Sum It All Up

Today you have already learned a lot about liking the child
you love. You've begun a very important and rewarding journey of self-discovery that will help you deepen and strengthen
your relationship with your child. Stay mindful of the following points as you continue this journey:

- Parenting is not easy, and wishing it would be easier makes it more difficult.
- We all, as parents, carry biases that shape our expectations.
- Both you and your child hurt when you see him in a negative light and when you get stuck in this biased and unfavorable mind-set.
- The key to having a good relationship with your child rests more with you than your child.
- The more you detoxify your thoughts about your child, the closer and less conflicted your relationship will be.

Chapter 2

Sliding Down the Slippery Slope of Toxic Thinking

Have you ever *really* considered what causes your parenting highs and lows? I have a shocking bulletin for you: It is not your difficult child propelling your ups and downs on the PFS roller coaster. Hold on, I'm not saying that your kid is an angel. I do get it. Kids provoke their parents. This leaves you feeling not only like a fish on a hook but also like a fish out of water. But just because your child floats those emotional hooks your way does not mean that you have to bite on them. In this chapter, I want to shed light on who is really in charge of how you feel and react—you.

Parents with more manageable children are usually those who are more successful at managing their own thoughts and emotions. That's right: The less stress and chaos *you* create in your mind, the easier it will be to be mindful of your child. And, this in turn, will make it far easier to get your child to mind you.

I am going to show you a more realistic, healthier, and more powerful way of thinking that will enhance your understanding of your child, improve communication with her, and solve problems. Truly understanding and effectively relating to your child is so crucial. It creates the solid foundation for working through those difficult times and also for a happier, closer relationship. The underlying secret to your parenting success can be found in one place and one place only—inside of you. And as I changed for the better, many parents in my practice have made those same positive changes, and so will you.

Let's now take a look at what I call toxic thinking.

Why Toxic Thinking Is a Serious Problem

My first book, *Why Can't You Read My Mind?* helps couples overcome the toxic thoughts that destroy intimacy and crush love. Intimate partners with toxic thoughts may think things like, "He is a selfish husband" or "She always has to be right." When couples fall prey to toxic thoughts, they can relentlessly wear down their ability to understand and love one another. Most distressed couples worry about falling out of love, but they might find it far more helpful to focus on how toxic thoughts erode *empathy*—the emotional glue that holds relationships of all kinds together.

Toxic thoughts that continue to build and fester can lead to breakups or even divorce. Sadly, many adults go on to form new intimate relationships in which they fall prey to similar types of consistently negative thoughts. As the saying goes, "Nothing changes if nothing changes."

Many readers have shared how much *Why Can't You Read My Mind?* helped them. It has been fulfilling to hear firsthand from so many couples who regained intimacy in their relationships. I have continued to see over and over in my psychology practice that intimate partners who learn how to control these toxic thoughts have more empathy and deeper, more lasting feelings of love.

Similar to the dynamics within couples, a damaging thinking process goes on between parents and their children. But when it comes to parenting, toxic thoughts seem much harder for people to tune in to and truly acknowledge. In this way, they may be even more damaging than in couples because they are often hidden or denied. After all, what parent wants to *really* admit what she says in the privacy of her mind when she gets upset with her child?

Denial is big. It is a very limiting force that holds us back from learning how to overcome challenges, including those we face as parents. Until we uproot it, we will repeat the same patterns ad infinitum. This chapter can help you feel safe enough to open up your mind to those dark, lurking thoughts that create a strain in your relationship with your child.

I have certainly fallen down as a parent at times as a result of my own toxic thoughts, especially when I denied them or consciously refused to deal with them. That's why I believe so strongly that once you take a good look at what goes on inside your mind, you'll be much better able to handle your child in those challenging times. Your self-awareness will pave the way to self-fulfillment as a parent and in every other realm of your life.

Parents who do not deal with their toxic thoughts have toxic feelings toward their children—which trigger negative emotions, which leave kids feeling misunderstood and alienated. It becomes a vicious cycle: Parent Frustration Syndrome. Clearly, it is very important for parents to get their own thoughts and emotions in order to meet the emotional needs of their children. Keep reading and you too will learn how.

Toxic Thoughts Can Permeate All Family Relationships

I'm not the only one who sees the similarities between thought patterns in intimate relationships and with your children. A client of mine, Rose, connected her toxic thinking in her marriage with her parenting. She and her husband, Terry, had seen me for couples' counseling a few years earlier, and she was also the mother of a defiant ten-year-old boy, Donny. One day, even more animated than usual, Rose declared a powerful insight: "Dr. Jeff, I can see myself repeating with Donny the same destructive thoughts I had with Terry. I could not believe how I had convinced myself that Terry and Donny were both insensitive human beings! Thankfully, it hit me like a ton of bricks when I realized that this was because of my distorted perceptions. My thoughts were really messing up my ability to see the challenges I faced with both my husband and my son. Now that I no longer convince myself that they are bad, I no longer see them in a bad way."

As Rose gained clarity and learned to see her husband and her son in a less toxic and less judgmental manner, she gained cooperation and respect from both of them. This breakthrough is one that you will achieve, too. As you will see, when you detoxify those thoughts, you give all those whom you love and value the chance to be seen (and also see you) in a more fair and balanced way.

Bonded for Life, for Better or Worse

The big catch in child rearing is that you don't have the same options to fly the coop that couples do. You and your children are bonded in this relationship for life. No matter what parents struggle with, they are still parents for all the years to come. Even though, at times, parents and children may share a fantasy of trading one another in, that's simply not possible. The bond between parent and child even goes on after our parents are no longer physically with us. As a parent myself, I can now see how my "voice" for better or worse will stay in my children's minds and hearts for the rest of their lives. If you recall, Exercise 2 from Chapter 1 helped you see this firsthand.

It is very clear that decades of psychological research and common sense tell us that strained and fractured parent-child relationships cause tremendous emotional distress for both sides. Here's how what's going on in your head affects the relationship between you and your child.

What Is Self-Talk?
And When Does It Turn Toxic?

Once you have children, your view on life profoundly changes. As a parent, you have a huge responsibility to nurture and raise your child to take care of herself. Your mind buzzes with thoughts about all the details of not only your own life but also your child's.

Parenting can offer so many joyful moments. But very often there are challenging times when we find ourselves resenting the pressures and challenges our children bring to us. What happens to make parents go from appreciating their kids to feeling like their kids are driving them out of their minds? I can answer that one for you: toxic thinking.

Toxic thoughts don't just pop up out of nowhere. In order to understand what toxic thinking is and how, like a cancer, it strains and eats away at parenting relationships, you must first understand what you do inside your head all day long, every single day of your life—you "self-talk."

So what is self-talk? Self-talk is all the thoughts that you have rattling through your brain all day long, those silent conversations you have with yourself as you go about your day. Conversations like, "I have to get Sarah and Jimmy to soccer and karate within twenty minutes of each other. Jimmy takes too darn long to get ready. I'm so overwhelmed. Why do I always get stuck in traffic? This is so stressful and unfair." Or "Why can't I plan things better when it comes to scheduling activities?" Or "I just don't know what I am going to do with this kid!" These are examples of self-talk. We all do it in our heads and even out loud once in a while. By the way, you're not crazy for—or alone in—talking to yourself like this.

Once you really tune in to your self-talk, you'll be astounded. You'll see how much self-talk you do—in the car, waiting in line at the supermarket, staring at your computer screen, or even when having lunch with friends. What's really amazing is how little we realize we're doing it.

The topics of your self-talk can be anything in your life: yourself, your kids, your dog, your job, or your intimate partner. Self-talk is simply another way that you process information. The key is seeing how your patterns of *how* you self-talk repeat themselves, no matter what the topic. It's like we have these internal memory discs that play on "repeat." Unless we make ourselves consciously aware of what they're saying, they just keep playing, and we unconsciously digest their tone and content endlessly.

And rest assured that self-talk is perfectly normal and healthy, even if it's occasionally negative. We all feel down or blue at times and look at things pessimistically, like "It's tough for me to get organized right now" or "I can't seem to get anything to go right today." Though these thoughts may be unpleasant, they are normal.

In many cases, negative self-talk can have some truth behind it. Maybe you really could have been more patient with your daughter or listened more effectively, and maybe you would look more attractive if you lost the weight you gained.

But there is a continuum of thought from positive to toxic. Toxic thoughts are negative thoughts that have lost connection with reality and gotten out of control. They cause you to lose your perspective. Unlike a thought such as "I wish I could more easily reach out and get closer to the other mothers in my neighborhood," toxic thoughts are twisted and distorted, like "I don't fit in with any of the other moms. They will just reject me, so what is the point of trying to make some new friends? Everyone thinks I am a lost cause."

The Self-Talk Continuum

Triggering Event	Positive Self-Talk (Healthy and Realistic)	Negative Self-Talk (Occasional, Realistic)	Toxic Self-Talk (Frequent, Black and White, Unrealistic)
You were late getting to your child's field day.	"Anyone can be late once in a while. I'll just need to be careful not to overextend myself so much in the mornings of school functions."	"I rushed too much and did not pay attention to prioritizing getting to the school on time."	"I can't seem to do anything right when it comes to showing up for my kids."
You screamed at your child.	"I am only human; it's just a reminder to pay attention to what I am thinking before I react to things."	"At times, I can really be loud and over the top."	"I can't even control my own temper and that makes me a lousy role model."
Your presentation at work received some negative feedback.	"This is a chance to try to learn from my mistakes and improve."	"This is because I did not take the time I needed to have been better prepared. I screwed up."	"I'll never measure up. I deserve to be fired."

The Consequences:
When Parental Thinking Gets Polluted

As you can see from "The Self-Talk Continuum," if your negative thoughts intensify and accelerate with momentum, life gets major-league miserable. When you begin to explain the events of your life in an all-encompassing, black-and-white style, you may have, without even realizing it, programmed your internal memory with upsetting, unpleasant, extreme thoughts about yourself and others. Too much negative self-talk will influence you to feel bad about yourself, others (including your child), and sometimes even the entire world. That's when self-talk has turned toxic. And this is what takes parents from mild to severe PFS, the state of mind where parents get into serious struggles with their challenging children.

When your thoughts turn increasingly pessimistic, you can easily fall prey to hopelessness—like believing you are a loser, your kids are only greedy bloodsuckers, or the world is one big place of misery. You may have also begun to tell yourself things like "I can't seem to manage my kids at all," "No parents struggle like I do," or "Being understanding to my kids means they will take advantage of me."

In the upcoming chapters I will show you how to conquer your toxic thoughts toward your child. Calming down, detecting, and zapping your toxic thoughts are crucial skills in becoming more even-keeled and effective as a parent. But hang on! Sorry to break this to you, but simply saying, "Okay, so all I have to do is become a positive thinker and life with my kids will be easier" is not going to cut it. I wish I could tell you it would. Of course, positive thoughts are helpful to have as you go through life—they really are. But as you will see, keeping a balanced parenting mind takes more than just having a positive parenting outlook.

All roads develop potholes the more they are traveled. Fortunately, there are crews out there to fill them to prevent damage to your car. Ensuring your healthy thought process also requires ongoing maintenance. Consider this book an essential guide to repairing the wear and tear of toxic thinking, preventing further damage to your relationships with your children, and paving the way to smoother travels.

Positive Parenting Takes More than Positive Thinking

Debbie, a client of mine, used to think of herself as a "positive parent," that is, before her kids became teenagers. The first time she consulted me was right after she and her husband and their two kids had come back from a ski vacation. Debbie recounted to me how she sat alone at the cabin, just wanting to be away from the chaos and melodrama of her thirteen-year-old daughter, Sydney. She had even repeatedly told herself, "I'm going to look at things with Sydney more positively." Unfortunately, Debbie's impromptu pep talk to herself was to no avail during their stay in Vail. Despite her best meditations and deep breaths, Debbie bit on the proverbial "hook" after Sydney muttered one too many times, "Mom-mmm, this vacation really sucks!" Debbie reflected to me, "Dr. Jeff, I screamed like a crazy woman to her about how she NEVER appreciates anything and that she had ALWAYS been a spoiled little brat. I guess I went a wee bit toxic, didn't I?"

As Debbie realized, even parents with a positive outlook can have tenuous relationships with their difficult children. I have had many positive-thinking parents end up in my office, surprised that they no longer feel the same ease with their children or teens. Why? Because when it comes to parenting, no one is immune.

Toxic thoughts toward our own children can include "You keep avoiding your homework, and you're going to throw your life away," "You keep making our family life impossible to enjoy," or "I can never believe anything you say because you always lie about where you are and what you are doing." Even though you love your child, you just don't like her when you think that way.

For obvious reasons, this is tricky to deal with. Most parents feel a profound sense of shame and embarrassment for thinking about their children in these ways. For many parents with more than one child, what compounds this guilt is that they have toxic thoughts more toward one child than the others. And these troublesome thoughts are very sneaky and insidious. Why? Because most of us fail to realize how often they occur outside of our awareness.

But don't worry—I'm going to show you surprisingly easy ways to become aware, to get the clues you need to control your toxic thinking instead of letting it control you. I'm also going to show you how, once armed with this special form of awareness—which I call parenting mindfulness—you can then learn easy-to-apply yet powerful strategies to dispute toxic thoughts. As you learn more about toxic thoughts, it will become clear why simply telling yourself "Okay, I'll just keep thinking positive about my child and it will get better" doesn't work. Trust me, if you do this, you'll fall flat on your face just like Debbie did. In fact, I bet you've already tried it. What you really need to do is grab those toxic thoughts and zap them. Toxic thoughts left to fester become only more poisonous and destructive. Remember: What you resist will persist.

Debbie was thrilled to hear that she wasn't going to find the answers to her problems by working even harder at her relationship with Sydney. She had to learn to work *smarter*. Simply isolating herself in the cabin and trying to convince herself that things would get better with her daughter left her feeling only more frustrated. After I worked with Debbie and her husband, they both learned some very powerful tools to feel better about and more satisfied with their children, including Sydney. I'm going to share those tools and the ones I have used with other clients with you. You'll have to do some work, but now you'll know how to work smart, not just hard.

Unrealistic Expectations Create Frustrations

Many parents have come into my office in tears of sadness and frustration, befuddled and distressed by a growing rift with their children. Once Debbie slowed down and identified and reviewed her toxic thoughts about her daughter, she was able to deal with her level of distress. The key is to take the time to first understand yourself and to clear out the toxic thoughts that block you from really being able to understand your child.

Stay with me—there is some great stuff coming to help you move way up your parenting-satisfaction meter. Yes, it will take some effort on your behalf. And yes, liking your unlikable child also takes energy. So have realistic expectations. The more that you expect it will take some work, the more likely it will work out for the better.

Sadly, many parents tend to think that parenting *should* be easier than it is, or that punishing their kids is the way to command respect. That's a nice fantasy, but far from the truth. Remember how I said earlier that *should* is a very problematic word? *Should* creates rigid expectations and feelings of shame when we, or others we apply it to, fall short of those expectations. In the words of Dr. Albert Ellis, please stop "shoulding" all over yourself and your child and strive for more manageable and realistic expectations. As you will see in Chapter 7, even replacing your *should*s with *would like* or *will consider* will ease pressures in your mind. Do this and you will feel a lot better.

As we go forward, you will further learn the power of being in control of your mind in ways you never imagined. I'm going to teach you a crucial lesson—how to really understand what your toxic thoughts are. I'm going to show you a very effective but surprisingly simple way to change the patterns in your mind. You will learn how to address your toxic thoughts every time they arise—and you won't believe how quickly your relationship with your child will improve. It really is amazing.

Let's first take a closer look at how self-talk works in your relationship with yourself.

Why Toxic Thinking Is So Hard to Catch

One of my clients, a woman named Charlotte, came to me because she was unhappy, even depressed. She was a struggling young mother with a colicky baby and a defiant six year old. Charlotte felt overwhelmed by her kids, had a job she said she hated, and was still overweight from her pregnancy. "I stink at life, and I'm basically a fat lost cause and a basket case," Charlotte declared at our first meeting.

When I explained what toxic thinking is and how it might be affecting Charlotte's ability to change her home and personal life, she quickly said, "Oh, no! I don't do that. My problem is that I'm depressed." Although Charlotte did have her fair share of depressed feelings, she first needed to understand how her own damaging self-talk created and fueled her negative feelings. To further clue her in, I provided Charlotte with written examples of toxic self-talk, similar to those below.

Examples of Toxic Self-Talk

- "If I fail, then I'm a worthless, no-good loser."
- "I am not good at anything."
- "Since my kids are not behaving well, I must be a lousy mother."
- "Parenting should be easy for me, like it is for my friends."
- "I should be a complete success in everything I do."
- "Those other fathers involved with the soccer team are better dads than I am."
- "In order to be a worthwhile human being, I need everyone's approval."
- "I can't bear disapproval from those who really care for me."
- "I can't do anything right."
- "I screw up everything in my life."
- "Those other moms just pretend they like me."
- "If people knew about my past failures, they would not respect me at all."

I then asked Charlotte to pay attention to her self-talk for one week and to write down what she was thinking. She came to our next session with a notebook. In it she had written her random thoughts, such as "You'll be in this job for the rest of your life because you didn't finish college," "You're now fat, and you'll never be able to lose the weight," and "You can't get Jimmy a playdate because you're not as together as the other mothers."

Charlotte was certainly surprised at her own thoughts. She had no idea how much of a toxic thinker she actually was. "Wow! I had no idea. It became such a habit, the way I kept thinking about myself and my life," said Charlotte, "I didn't even know I was doing it!"

Why Toxic Self-Talkers Find Parenting Stressful

Charlotte was making herself miserable, sabotaging her self-esteem and assertiveness. So it may not surprise you that she would have difficulty parenting with the same tainted outlook. With her toxic thoughts driving her along, Charlotte kept overreacting, then punishing herself by putting herself down and eating excessively to console herself.

Children won't behave well for parents who are haunted by their own troubled thoughts. This is because these thoughts block parents from understanding their children and tuning in to their emotional needs. Though she loved her children, Charlotte's self-esteem was so poor that she was scared her children would be as helpless as she felt she was. There are many toxic self-talkers with poor self-esteem who do raise children—but it is not surprising that these kids tend to suffer.

Was toxic thinking the only problem Charlotte needed to work on? No, certainly not. Her kids and other life challenges were demanding, that was for sure. But what was going on in her head was a big part of her problem. Eliminating the toxic thoughts has helped her change her life in many positive ways. It wasn't always easy, and it did take her some time, but Charlotte is now a happier parent.

Parents who are prone to PFS will likely have a hard time relating clearly, reasonably, and open-mindedly to their children. Why? Because you can't relate well to your kids if you can't relate well to yourself. Let's not stop here. The old saying "You have to love yourself before you can love anyone else" is absolutely true. As you will soon see, in so many cases our toxic thoughts about our kids are not even really *about* our kids; they are about our own "stuff." Our childhood experiences, commonly referred to as past "baggage," or "emotional ghosts," often lead us to have unrealistic expectations, or "hot buttons," that fuel our toxic thoughts toward our children.

The Causes of Toxic Self-Talk

The triggers are usually urgently wanting your child to do something she is not doing, such as listen better, be more active, have more friends, or get good grades. Or your distress is sparked by not wanting your child to do what she is doing, such as talking back to you, getting poor grades, making a mess of her room, or picking on a sibling.

Adults' childhood experiences often play out in the attitudes they have toward their own children. Parents who were told as children, for example, that they were irresponsible may struggle with responsibility as a parent. Those told that they were lazy may be too permissive with their own kids because they are afraid of overly pressuring them. Parents who were labeled as "the one with the looks" may overly stress the value of their own child's attractiveness. The list can go on and on. The important point is to tune in to the impact and influence of these dynamics. To be sure, past does not necessarily mean future. Adults can and do transform their past negative, self-limiting perceptions and grow in positive directions. But in most cases, doing so takes self-awareness and effort.

Let me make it clear that low parental self-esteem is not the only factor that causes toxic thinking. I truly believe that the vast majority of parents get toxic thoughts, to varying degrees, toward their children. Some parents may have great self-esteem but have a difficult time understanding why their own children are so difficult or different from them. Other parents may be overloaded by the demands of a child with anxiety, depression, attention deficit hyperactivity disorder (ADHD), or plain old moodiness.

But I'm Not a Toxic Self-Talker!

You may be thinking, "Well, Dr. Jeff, this book isn't for me because it is my child who is the real problem. I'm not a toxic self-talker." A parent may tell me, "Look, how I *think* about my child isn't my problem," and then go though a litany of things they don't like about their child (remember my "Top-Ten List of What Parents Don't Like About Their Children" in Chapter 1?). I understand the skepticism. But after they are done venting, I supportively share with them that toxic thinking is most likely a factor in their PFS, especially if they're not able to sit down and truly talk things out with their child or teen. And by the way, giving a lecture or yelling does not count as talking things out. The bottom line is that if you have problems discussing concerns with your child, difficulty in resolving conflicts, or frequently find yourself screaming at your child, toxic thinking is probably getting in the way of your relationship.

Realize that you can still be a toxic thinker when it comes to your child, even if your thoughts about yourself are rarely that negative. Perhaps you generally avoid toxic thinking in your marriage or even with difficult colleagues at work. What throws many mothers and fathers off balance, however, is that their toxic thoughts may be *mostly* directed toward their child. This reality is scary, and hard for many parents to admit.

Try writing down any strong negative thoughts you may have about yourself and your child. When I send my clients home with this exercise, most of them discover they are indeed prone to thinking toxically. This is what gets in the way of liking this child whom you love so much.

Questioning If You're a Toxic Thinker? Take the Self-Talk Challenge and Find Out!

You may not think you're a toxic self-talker. You may be a positive self-talker who has very healthy self-esteem. I hope so. But it's possible that you are a toxic self-talker and **you just don't know it**. Before deciding, please tune in to hear what you're thinking about yourself and your child. You may be in for a big surprise.

This exercise is simple. For a few days, remind yourself to listen to your internal tapes. Every time you catch yourself thinking something about yourself or your child, write it down on a piece of paper with the following headings:

Table 2.1   Thoughts you have about yourself

Positive (Healthy, Realistic Despite Problems/Obstacles)	Negative (Occasional Gray Area)	Toxic (Frequent Black-and-White Thoughts)
Example: "I'm doing well today in spite of my daughter being moody and difficult."	Example: "Lately, I just wish my family life would be easier."	Example: "I can never manage the kids without losing it and making all of our lives miserable."

Table 2.2   Thoughts you have about your child

Positive (Healthy, Realistic Despite Problems/Obstacles)	Negative (Occasional Gray Area)	Toxic (Frequent Black-and-White Thoughts)
Example: "She may be more sensitive and it helps me to remember that."	Example: "I wish she was not so challenging. It really gets to me sometimes. "	Example: "There she goes again. All she wants is to make me miserable."

As you do this exercise, remember that the difference between negative thinking and toxic thinking is intensity and frequency. If you splurge and eat a hot fudge sundae during your favorite television show and feel bad about yourself for hours or days afterward ("I'm a fat slob"), that's toxic thinking. If your daughter is late for school and you're telling yourself, "Maybe we need to reevaluate the morning readiness routine," that's a positive way to explain her lateness. But if you jump to the conclusion that "she just can't take care of herself and will never make it in the real world and hold down a job," you're summing your teen up in a strongly negative and most likely inaccurate way. You're describing not a situation or experience but instead your global and negative interpretation of your child's concerns.

Your Mind Has a Powerful
Influence over How You Feel

Toxic thinking has such a powerful impact because *your toxic thoughts profoundly influence how you feel and react.* This is one of the most important points to understand. The thoughts we think when we talk to ourselves don't simply go in and out of our heads. They stick. Our feelings, moods, and actions are driven by our self-talk. I'm sure you have heard yourself or someone you know say, "I don't know why, but I feel so much more patient with him today" or "I can't figure out why I'm so angry at my daughter." There's no mystery: This is proof of the power of your underlying self-talk. Your thoughts can make you feel either good about your child or disappointed, angry, or sad.

If you're telling yourself over and over again that your daughter is irresponsible and lazy, what feelings are you going to have about her? Bad ones! You're going to feel like you're stuck with an irresponsible, lazy child—maybe for life.

If your internal self-talk memory disc has "She's bringing down this whole family" on constant "play," you will end up focusing on all of those events or experiences in your life that prove to you that she is. You are going to feel bad about yourself for letting her make your family life miserable. And what kind of relationship with your child can you have with these types of thoughts swirling around in your head? Not a very strong one.

You can also make yourself physically sick. A colleague once shared with me a quote that read, "Our bodies weep the tears that our eyes refuse to shed." I have had parents in my office complaining of stomach ailments, skin rashes, and migraines all because family tensions had reached sky-high limits. If you're a toxic self-talker, you might have high blood pressure, difficulty sleeping, or a compulsive eating problem. No doubt about it, when we think and talk toxic, we feel toxic—stressed out, tired, and oftentimes depressed and anxious.

So even if you don't realize you're telling yourself something toxic about your child, toxic talk still influences the way you feel and behave. If you tell yourself something toxic about your child day after day, or during challenging situations, eventually you will perceive that as the reality—even if it's not. So now that you are beginning to understand how these thought patterns impact you, stop beating yourself up for having them.

Toxic Thinking Creates Its Own Reality

The overlooked truth about toxic thinking is that it shapes our experiences—*even if the thoughts are not based in reality.* That's a powerful statement. It's also scary, isn't it? We can turn our thoughts into reality—thoughts that we may not even be aware we're having!

This means that even if we're not bad parents or parents who lack control, we can actually convince ourselves, and therefore others, that we *are* just by thinking such a thing about ourselves. Or that if in the big picture your child has many strengths but you focus on her weaknesses, then you will see her in an unfairly negative manner. That is big-time scary!

Toxic Thoughts Drive Toxic Behaviors in Families

Over and over I have seen families at a breaking point, often with one or both parents or the kids feeling anxious or depressed, turning to food, alcohol, drugs, destructive relationships, or pornography for comfort. Most of the time, toxic thinking is an important contributor, if not the main contributor, to these problems. Typically, these families have come to therapy only after their toxic thoughts have been slamming them around for years.

Toxic thoughts often incite parents to behave toxically toward their children. They may even "lose it," seemingly out of the blue.

This can include mocking, embarrassing, yelling at, bullying, threatening, humiliating, lying to, giving the silent treatment to, and even hitting their children. As one teen shared with me, "It's like they get all this crap about me buzzing in their heads. Then my parents 'spaz out' and say mean things to me."

It is heart-wrenching for me to see parents unable to make the connection between their toxic thoughts and their problematic parenting behaviors. Parent-child relationships suffer greatly when parents think and behave toxically in response to their children.

Control Your Toxic Thoughts Before They Control You

The power of our thoughts has been examined by philosophers and psychologists for a very long time. Socrates said, "The unexamined life is not worth living," and Roman philosopher Epictetus had this epiphany: "Man is not disturbed by events alone but by his *perception* of events." Or in the Buddha's words, "What you think, you become." Yet every time I see clients realize the power of their own minds, it is nonetheless profound.

Following the wisdom of these great scholars, doesn't it stand to reason that it is possible to detoxify our thinking and change our perception of events? This has also been a cornerstone of modern psychology. Imagine the freedom we could enjoy if we stopped sabotaging ourselves and our parenting efforts. Think how much better we'd all feel if we could deal with the real issues with our children instead of our distorted, toxic perceptions.

The truth is you can actually feel better by modifying how you think about yourself. So instead of thinking that you are "being irresponsible," think that you made an "honest mistake," or had a "key learning experience." Instead of "being lazy," you took a "recharging period." Instead of "being a failure," you had a "setback" or are "closer to a solution."

Yes, becoming a more mindful, healthier thinker takes some work. In this light (no pun intended) think of Thomas Edison, inventor of the lightbulb, who said, "I have not failed. I've just found 10,000 ways that won't work." And we all know that making a lightbulb is probably much easier than raising a child!

Don't you think you would start feeling differently about yourself if you could detoxify your mind? Absolutely! And don't you think you would start to feel better about your child if you could detoxify your thinking about him? Absolutely yes to this question too!

Learning how to rethink and work through your toxic thoughts is key to feeling good about yourself *and* others. It's also the key to making positive changes. By applying the new set of more healthy, realistic, and positive thinking skills that you will learn in the chapters ahead, you will be able to rid your life of the toxic thoughts that are undermining your ability to be a calm, centered parent.

But What If I Can't Get Rid of My Toxic Thinking?

You *can* learn to rethink the frustrating and stressful situations in your life—especially with your children. So if you're surprised or bummed out to discover that you're a toxic thinker, don't panic. I've worked with parents with pretty serious cases of toxic thinking, and they've been able to break the habit, for the simple reason that they tuned in, wanted to change, and remained committed to sticking with the changes. You have tremendous mental recourses and a huge capacity for self-awareness. If you were walking on the sidewalk with your child and a car was swerving toward your child, would you grab your child and protect him? Of course you would. This is *mindfulness*. In Chapter 5 I will show you ways to become more mindful so you can be on the lookout for your toxic thoughts.

The tools presented in this book will help you behave and even feel differently about yourself, your situation, and the people in your life. Imagine the possibilities! No more being overwrought by PFS. By thinking differently, instead of "I'm so angry I could hang my daughter out to dry," you can be "peeved" at her. Rather than seeing your son as a "liar," you can see him as "not feeling safe to be honest with you." But I'm not talking about simply changing words; I'm talking about changing perceptions and feelings.

It all comes down to a simple yet powerful realization. There is no question about it: ***The way we think about events in our lives directly influences how we feel about them and ourselves—for better or worse.*** The good news is that we can control our behavior by controlling our thoughts and feelings. When you apply this new set of thinking skills to parenting, you'll be surprised at how it will bring you and your child even closer. You'll feel more connected and have more mutual understanding than you ever imagined.

To Sum It All Up

Today you reached a startling realization. You have learned how your thoughts, for better or worse, play a huge role in shaping your attitudes and actions as a parent. I admire your courage to look within yourself and consider new ways to make that all-important, lasting positive difference in your child's life. Please keep the following points in mind as we go forward:

- Your mind drives how easy or hard it is for you to mind your child.
- We all self-talk, and our self-talk shapes our feelings in response to our children.

- Toxic thoughts about our children, within our awareness or not, do not elude the awareness of our children.
- Your success in parenting is strongly driven by how you view and react to your child, especially when she is challenging.
- You have the freedom to choose how you think, feel, and react to your child, and although it will take some time, this will be easier than you ever imagined.

Chapter 3

Recognizing the Nine Toxic-Thought Patterns of Parenting

A WOMAN NAMED LORRAINE came in to see me for a consultation a few years ago. The mother of an angry and spiteful fourteen-year-old girl, she was at the end of her rope. "She just takes, takes, and takes more from me, and I don't have any more to give," Lorraine said. "She is ungrateful and mean, and I wish someone else could take care of her."

As you can well imagine, the last thing Lorraine wanted to hear was how thinking differently would be the most important step to making things better. After all, wasn't it her kid with the behavioral problem? Lorraine actually was quite upset with me at first. "Sure, Dr. Jeff, you met her, and she was charming with you, just like she is to everyone else. But she is horrible with me. And you're asking *me* to be the one to change?!"

I let Lorraine vent. And then, with my encouragement, she did something she never thought she would do. Over the next week, she looked at her thoughts, at all the negative crap she was feeding herself about her daughter, and discovered something powerful: The more she took ownership of what she was telling herself, the more her daughter trusted and opened up to her.

You see, it is very hard to listen to a child when you are filling yourself with your own toxic chatter. But when you open up your mind and your heart, when you lead with understanding and put your ego on the shelf, wonderful rewards await you.

Many moms and dads have come out on the other side, as Lorraine did. What they all initially shared is the feeling of being overwhelmed. They had racing thoughts and feelings of distress and despair when dealing with their children. But instead of waiting for their kids to become "better kids" or even make better choices, they first chose to look at their own attitudes—specifically, how they had chosen to think of their kids in toxic ways.

It's time to shine some light on those dark thoughts that clamor inside your brain. The light is self-awareness. Once you know exactly what these vexing thoughts are, and learn how to manage them, you will lower your PFS. Just hang on, stay with me, and you will see.

Yes, I will be challenging you in this chapter. I am pushing you to go somewhere new. You may feel it's scary to face your toxic-thought patterns. Why wouldn't it be? We are talking about how you think and feel about your child! But the alternative is much worse. Those lurking toxic thoughts are far more dangerous than those that are uncovered, dealt with, and put to rest. For example, you may find yourself saying to your friend or spouse, "I feel so burned out with my kids, like I can't handle any more right now" or "I don't know why I just screamed at him out of the blue." Like waters swelling against a dam, toxic thoughts build up. Sometimes they gradually weigh you down with resentment, sadness, or agitation. Others are likely to erupt in explosive outbursts. But soon, you will no longer say, "I wish I knew how to not get so stressed out from my kids," because you *will* know how.

Denial may seem tempting, but it comes with a price. It's easy to view these thoughts as harmless because they occur in the privacy of your mind and to want to convince yourself that your child can't really sense them. But remember what I said about kids having their own radar? When kids sense your negative vibes, they will often shut down and distance themselves, or they will find some way to act out and rebel.

Remember, again, that *you are not alone*. Most parents are besieged with toxic thoughts; they just don't realize it. As I mentioned earlier, you probably feel that you are not supposed to think of your child in any kind of negative manner. I realize that you are trying so hard to be a "good" parent or you would not be reading this book. Let me assure you that wrestling with toxic thoughts makes you a normal and caring parent. As you will learn, it is what you do, or don't do, with these thoughts that determines whether you are an *effective* parent.

Yes, it will take some work to overcome your toxic thoughts. You're making a giant leap forward in self-awareness and self-control. But compared to dealing with escalating tensions and increased misunderstandings, this work is a breeze. Trust me, based on my experience with many misunderstood children and frustrated parents, it's worth the effort.

You Have More Control than You Think

Caring for children has been studied extensively and scientifically. And powerful caring feelings toward our young can be traced to what is called the midbrain. This part of the brain helps to navigate our emotions, attention, motivation, empathy, decision making, and the other functions of complex thinking required to maneuver through the intricacies of parenting. How we tune in and emotionally connect to our children is no doubt hardwired. But as you will see, our brains are also flexible enough to learn new thought patterns.

It is important to keep in mind that most research suggests that the human brain is not fully developed until we are in our early to midtwenties. Thus, as adults, we have more control over our thoughts and emotions than our children do. Although it is imperative to have reasonable behavioral standards for your child, it is just as crucial to remember that you are the one with the fully developed brain. This is why it is so important for you to set an example of healthy thinking and reacting. Beyond the way we are wired, we also have a set of beliefs upon which we base our parenting decisions, including societal attitudes, our family of origin's viewpoints, and our personal opinions.

Between our brain physiology and our beliefs, you may want to believe that the way you think as a parent is pretty much set in stone. I could not disagree more! In their book *The Mind and the Brain*, Jeffrey Schwartz and Sharon Begley share that people with obsessive compulsive disorder changed their brain activities and physiologies by learning new ways of thinking. It is quite notable that those reported brain changes were just as significant for those taking medication as those who did not. Similar results have been shown with depression and anxiety. I have also seen over and over in my psychology practice and in the feedback from readers of my books that parents can absolutely change their parenting attitudes and behaviors—much for the better!

Most exciting is that when parents change their ways of thinking, their children respond differently. What got me in trouble in my early days as a father was that I *rigidly* held to the idea that my job was to be "in charge" of my kids. This belief led me to be controlling and dominating. I eventually discovered that this simply led my children to resent and resist me. Because of my delivery, they missed the message that I had their best interests in mind—and their defiant behavior would escalate. But as I changed my emphasis from commanding to understanding, wonderfully positive changes occurred. If I did it, so can you! As you learn to stay clearheaded, supportive, and constructive with your children, the more your children will grow emotionally strong and healthy.

Keep in mind that each of us has our own threshold for toxic thinking. Some parents may fall into it more readily than others.

For example, one mother who steps over three backpacks and three pairs of shoes may be irritated but not get too riled up. Yet another mom may find that despite her impromptu fancy footwork, she finds herself revving with PFS.

Now we are going to flip on those bright lights that I mentioned at the beginning of this chapter. Below are the descriptions of the nine toxic-thought patterns. You will likely discover yourself in one or more of these patterns. It's just as common, however, not to "see it" until you're having an issue with your child. Wham! Suddenly, you are in the middle of an argument and find yourself thinking, "Okay, this seems familiar."

I have had many shocked parents share with me that they are, in their words, "guilty" of having one, two, or even all of the nine toxic-thought patterns buzzing around in their heads. Remember, you are not on trial for having these thoughts, at least not in my book (no pun intended)! Nor are we shooting for perfection. Realize too that we all vary in what bogs us down. Don't worry about how many, or which, of the toxic thoughts you identify with. Simply read them over with an open mind and see which ones resonate with you. In the later chapters you will learn how to relax your mind, how to become mindful enough to "catch" your toxic thinking as it occurs, and concrete strategies to overcome your toxic-thinking patterns for the long haul.

The Nine Toxic Thoughts of Parenting

Here they are: the nine toxic-thought patterns that make parenting quite painful. The first five are the thoughts that tend to build over time, and the remaining four are more prone to result in angry outbursts. Please note that this list is not rigid or absolute. Some of the less reactive toxic thoughts may flare up faster at times, and some of the more reactive ones may be more contained.

Slow-Burning Toxic Thoughts

1. The "Always or Never" Trap

Julie was one exasperated mom. She struggled with her thirteen-year-old daughter, Rachel, who had driven her to try everything from yoga to meditation to kickboxing. Julie wanted to find relief from Rachel's lack of appreciation and dramatic outbursts. Ever the dutiful mom, Julie rubbed Rachel's head at night before she went to sleep. She listened to Rachel complain about how all her teachers were unfair and how the other seventh-grade girls were bitches. And between Rachel and her two younger sisters, Julie felt like she did enough laundry to fill a Laundromat!

Julie's mind became infested with toxic thoughts. Julie lost sight of Rachel's good days because they were overshadowed by her reactions to Rachel's bad days. As Julie got locked into the "always or never" trap, she became increasingly fed up. "Dr. Jeff, this girl is never satisfied with anything I do for her. She always creates drama in our house. Rachel never cares about anyone but herself. I finally get so worn down that I just give in."

This is the language of the destructive "always or never" trap, the tendency of parents to see their kids completely negatively. For example, "He *never* tries in school." Or "She's *always* picking on her younger brother." Or "He *never* gives in when I try to reason with him." The reality is that "always or never" is inaccurate. I know it *feels* that way, but do your child's problem behaviors really go on for twenty-four hours a day, seven days a week? I doubt it.

Yet as you read this you may say, "But Dr. Jeff, it really does feel that way." I know it does. But realize you are in the throes of Parent Frustration Syndrome. The reason your child seems to *always* do the wrong thing or *never* does the right thing is because your perceptions are distorted. The reality is that most kids display a range of behaviors. Yet it is the work of our "always or never" toxic thoughts that lead us to unfavorably exaggerate our children's undesirable ones.

When human beings feel hurt or otherwise upset, there are a lot of instances of "always" and "never" that fly around in their heads and spill out of their mouths. (Heck, sometimes I fall into the "always and never" trap with parents I try to help. I have to make sure I don't start believing that all the parents in my practice *always* complain or *never* focus on their children's positive strengths!) I can tell you, based on hours and hours of listening to distressed and exasperated parents, that the "always or never" toxic-thought problem is, without a doubt, the most pervasive of all.

Why do we fall into the "always or never" habit in the first place? To reduce our emotional stress and tension. Consider what you say to yourself when your child's statements or actions don't make sense (*How could he not know that always forgetting to flush the toilet drives me crazy?*) or when your child doesn't cooperate (*She never cleans her room without first having a major war with me*). You need to find a way to make sense of this maddening stuff. And "always or never" thinking gives us the illusion that the problem is not fixable. It is the language of giving up and losing faith, which precludes constructive problem solving.

Be assured, I realize all this angst arises only because you so desperately want to prepare your child to "make it" in the world and be happy. Ironically, stressing about this can make you and your child miserable. When you explain to yourself why your child is being so difficult, "always or never" thinking is a very tempting place to go. But it is far more destructive than protective. When you think about your child as "You always . . . " or "You never . . . ," you create a wider and wider gap in your ability to understand him. And if you verbalize these thoughts, I can practically guarantee that your child's eyes will roll!

So if you're putting your daughter on trial with "You never listen" or "You always take the easy way out," she will inevitably become defensive or avoidant or will completely shut down. The inevitable return volley (either internalized or expressed) of "You always pick on me the most" or "Nothing I do is ever good

enough" then ensues instead of productive discussion and problem solving.

Success in parenting comes from seeing your child's behaviors
on a continuum of strengths and weaknesses. Raising an emotionally healthy, self-reliant child is not about how you expect him
to be but rather about being able to accept him for who he wants
to be. By spotting those toxic thoughts of always and never, you are
now on the way to helping your child grow into a healthy, realized
adult.

2. Label Gluing

"He's lazy." "She's insensitive." "He's a liar." "She's a drama queen."
Oh, those toxic, insidious labels. They sure can be damaging to
children. Labels can grow out of "always or never" thinking when
parents begin to view their children in a fixed way. Sadly, the adage
"Give a child a label and he lives up to it" is true. Toxic labels tend
to demotivate children from making positive changes.

Gus, the father of seventeen-year-old Lenny, thought his son
was lazy. Yet Lenny had a black belt in karate, was popular with his
peers at school, and held a part-time job at the local supermarket.
His grades, however, were poor. The reality is that Lenny was likely
heading for community college, and Gus was very disappointed
about this. Lenny simply did not have the same aptitude for aca-
demics that Gus did. The easiest way for Gus to process this difference in his own mind was to glue the label of lazy on Lenny.

Being on the lookout for your child's problematic behaviors
makes sense. But labeling your child because of them makes no
sense whatsoever. Children tend to live up—or down—to our expectations. So if you say, "Peter's our whiner" or "Tracy's our shy
child," then what may have been a phase becomes part of a more
permanent identity. This is much more damaging to a child's self-
concept than some parents realize, and it perpetuates the very behavior you find so objectionable!

I encourage you to pay attention to how toxic labeling creates a life of its own. Parents often resort to labeling because they have no other way of explaining why their children are misbehaving or falling short of expectations. Don't get me wrong—I realize that some labels can be innocuous and even endearing. For example, I know a mother of an energetic five-year-old boy whom she affectionately named Bamm-Bamm (after the Flintstones' well-intended yet overzealous toy-busting child). That's different, however, from labeling a five year old as "my problem child" because he does not fit in with peers at an early kindergarten program.

So why, whether in their own minds or out loud, do parents label their kids? Well, labels are another easy and convenient way to process information. Labels, like other toxic thoughts, germinate in the minds of parents who are fraught with frustration, anger, and resentment.

This may not seem evident, but at times the labels parents project onto their children reflect areas of dissatisfaction in the parents themselves. I know at times when I struggled with my own kids and labeled them toxically that I was not feeling so great about myself. For example, when I struggled with my own organizational issues, it was much easier to pick on my kids for having similar problems than to face my own.

At times labels can lead parents to become overly suspicious of their children's motives or behaviors. For example, a broken dish may have been knocked over by the baby or the cat, but the clumsy preteen is often the first one blamed. This dynamic will be further explained separately under the toxic thought of "blame blasting."

Recently, Jane, a high school senior with ADHD, sat in my office with her parents. Jane's dad, Ralph, had labeled her as careless and irresponsible in response to her academic shortcomings. Jane subsequently became pregnant. At that point, the last thing Jane needed to hear was that she was doomed to being careless and irresponsible, especially from her own father. Jane, however, had the baby and stepped up to a level of responsibility that astounded her father. Jane rose above her nonflattering labels. Although some children may overcome the self-fulfilling prophesies on their own, why keep labeling them and risk otherwise?

Another form of toxic labeling occurs when a parent negatively identifies a child with a spouse, an ex-spouse, or a sibling, telling the child, "You're just like your father" or "Why do you have to be so much like your mother?"

Finally, bear in mind, too, that some labels start out in a playful manner. In a recent family session, a shapely fifteen-year-old girl shared with her father that his calling her "chesty" was no longer amusing. Fortunately, the father had humility and smarts. He took responsibility for his loose, inappropriate humor and nipped it in the bud. We have heard the expression "Many a truth is spoken in jest." The problem is that parents often underestimate the emotional weight that labels, even humorous ones, carry in the eyes of their children. Children, by definition, are developing beings. Their self-esteem is developing, too, and toxic labels can upset the development of this all-important sense of self-worth. The more you watch out for toxic labels, the more you will avoid their pitfalls.

3. Seething Sarcasm

Kenny loved joking around with his fifteen-year-old daughter, Bridgette. He figured it was a way to use humor to get his point across and let off some PFS steam at the same time. In fact, Kenny often thought of himself as a "cool dad." What Kenny did not realize, however, was that his cutting thoughts, comments, and behaviors were actually upsetting his daughter. It was not until one of Bridgette's friends told Kenny the truth about why Bridgette was crying one day that he realized his sarcasm had such a negative impact.

Parents use sarcasm when they say things they don't fully mean, make mocking exaggerations, or imply the opposite of what they're saying through their tone of voice. For example, a parent says something like "Oh, aren't *you* graceful" when a child breaks something.

The use of sarcasm hurts children. Rarely is it a useful tool for effective communication. A thirteen-year-old client once said, "When my parents get sarcastic, they are just being jerks. They think they are being funny, and I hate it."

By definition, sarcasm is caustic. As with anything caustic, you need to handle it carefully to avoid destructive results. I've witnessed two major problems related to children and parental sarcasm. First, sarcasm can hurt feelings, and words uttered in a "humorous moment" can continue to cause pain later. Parents who communicate by issuing a steady flow of sarcasm can expect casualties. Ideally, I suggest completely curtailing the sarcasm. Or if you are not up for a moratorium, you need healthy boundaries. Give your children the right to tell you it bothers them, and respect that. Don't be too proud to apologize, even if it seems like no big deal to you. As you pay attention to where the boundaries are, get into the habit of living within them.

The second pitfall is more subtle. Sarcasm can mask sensitive or vulnerable feelings. Here, too, the result may be pain and conflict. Imagine a father watching his lovely sixteen-year-old daughter come downstairs. He might say, "Honey, you look beautiful tonight," or he might quip, "Man, you were such a homely little girl. What happened?" The underlying point may be the same, but one hides the compliment in an insult.

Elsa appreciated how her partner, Delores, helped her see how she had become sarcastic toward her thirteen-year-old son, Ben. Elsa had met Delores two years earlier, a year after she had come out and gotten a divorce from her husband. While Ben was becoming more accepting of his mother's lesbian lifestyle, he still struggled with it. At times he would make some nasty comments under his breath, which drove Elsa nuts. Elsa loved Ben and tried to be patient. But one day after Ben muttered "Les be friends," Elsa's PFS quotient sent her seething. She decided to give Ben a dose of his own medicine and get sarcastic with him. She mocked his performance at a recent baseball game: "Ben, thank God my life did not depend on the way you pitched tonight." Later that night, Ben broke down in tears and shared with Elsa how scared he was that his friends would tease him because his mother was involved with Delores. Both agreed to curb their sarcastic words. Using the strategies in Chapter 6, Elsa put her sarcastic thoughts to rest, and Ben followed her example.

Remember that as a parent you'll reap what you sow. You may not like that. You may call your "style" sarcastic, but when it comes back at you from your child or teen, you'll probably call it "disrespectful."

4. Smoldering Suspicions

Latasha had been growing increasingly defiant with her mother, Lavern. Things hit an all-time low, however, when Lavern noted one morning that she was missing $165 from her wallet. As her mind raced, she thought, "This girl can't be trusted." She became more anxious, thinking, "My possessions are not safe in my own house." It was only later that Lavern recalled that she had used her cash to buy groceries the night before. By that time, Latasha had already read the note Lavern had left saying she had to pay back the money she had "stolen," and the girl was justifiably upset.

Parents prone to "smoldering suspicions" face major challenges trusting their children. Parents who fall prey to them have trouble controlling their anxiety and have a need for control. Doubts that fuel their suspicions can set off the spark of feeling out of control. So this is how the vicious cycle of suspicion works. The benefit of the doubt gets swallowed up. The more anxiety a parent struggles with, the more trust is eroded. Smoldering suspicions can be fueled by label gluing, especially when labels have a theme of distrust, as in "liar" or "untrustworthy." This toxic thought becomes even more problematic in the teen years when kids become more elusive.

Ten-year-old Ginger was a budding artist. Phillip, her dad, was very happy she attended art classes and nurtured her talent. When he saw paint on the new couch, however, Phillip was not so supportive. As he started to tell Marina, his wife, that Ginger needed to be more careful with her paints, Marina revealed that the accidental couch art award went to the neighbor's three-year-old child. Phillip realized his suspicions were wrong.

In another example, eleven-year-old Dale was very upset when he was wrongfully accused of provoking his younger sister, Andrea. She had mastered a sad face, and their dad, Tim, fell easily into her trap. After overhearing Andrea brag to her friend on the phone that she got Dale in trouble, Tim felt very upset with himself for reaming Dale out.

Now, it may be true that your child has indeed been behaving in ways that make it difficult to trust him. And, unfortunately, some kids do get in patterns of operating in a devious manner. I have seen innumerable children elude parents' attempts to monitor their every move. Kids can be very resourceful. I have learned of secret marijuana apparatuses stored in floor vents, secret trips out into the night, stolen money, sexual acting out, and many other crafty escapades. Building trust comes best by keeping your cool and expressing disapproval without being harsh and shaming. Yes, you are only human and once in while you may lose it and yell, but striving to have more control over yourself will help you feel more in control of whatever challenges you are facing with your child. This certainly may take longer than jumping to conclusions, but it works far better at getting the truth than giving in to smoldering suspicions.

Should your child's devious behaviors escalate, then you may need to take direct action. For example, around the time of this writing, I encouraged a father of an ever-elusive teen girl in my practice to report her to the principal after she skipped school a second time. To the father's credit, he told his daughter he was taking this action, yet he used a newfound supportive tone versus his more usual accusatory one. Keep in mind that some kids who are deceitful may be actually crying out for help, and in those cases counseling can be quite helpful as well.

5. Detrimental Denial

Dennis, age twelve, was the target of teasing among other sixth graders. He was smaller than his peers, and that did not help matters. Yet what truly seemed to spark the teasing problems was Dennis's development of a "big mouth" to make up for his small physical stature. For example, Dennis had made up a rumor that a boy in his class "made out" with a girl whom he referred to as a "slut." Dennis could not seem to resist inventing these types of stories, and this was a huge obstacle to his blending in and making friends.

Dennis's father, Gary, was a seasoned attorney, and he was also on the school board. Gary made it no secret that he strived to be "super-dad," and he was on a mission to show his ex-wife that their son was innocent of what he was accused of. Dennis then played the nasty-rumor game in his Boy Scout troop. At that point, however, Gary wisely stopped his denial and supported Dennis's getting some outside counseling. Fortunately, Dennis was able to talk through and sort out his underlying anxieties and self-esteem issues. Gary was able to shed his thick skin of denial and more realistically see his son's struggles and be supportive. This also paved the way for a better working coparenting relationship with his ex-wife.

"Detrimental denial" is very different from the other toxic thoughts. The other eight are common to parents struggling with critical and negative thoughts about their children. Detrimental denial, however, occurs when instead of feeling excess frustration about the child's struggles or problems, a parent makes excuses for them. Parents with detrimental denial convince themselves that things are perfect with their kids when this is far from the case.

Over the years I have seen a lot of parents in detrimental denial. These parents distort reality to deflect emotional pain. I have heard many parents trying to convince me that their child's problems are the fault of his teacher, school, peers, coach, or sibling. The denial feels comforting for these parents. Bypassing the child's need to take responsibility leaves the other party always at fault. But then the parent's perceptions become erroneous and laden with fantasy. Rarely are a child's problems exclusively the fault of others. Even in cases of bullying, there are ways that children can be taught to avoid or minimize being victims (I have included some books on this topic in the "Recommended Reading" section at the end of this book).

Although it might feel natural to blame others in your child's life for his problems, this strategy usually makes things worse. The words *if only* are red flags in detrimental denial. If you think or make these types of statements, then you are likely in dangerous denial: "It's not her fault. If only the teacher would be more patient, she would be doing better" or "If only the coach would have given her a chance." A shifting of blame, such as "She never would have hit her if someone had told her not to move," is also a clear sign of denial.

You may be wondering, "What about times when my kid is not treated fairly by others?" Yes, once in a while you may find situations where you absolutely must protect and advocate for your child. But providing valid intervention on behalf of your child is far different from a pattern of distortion and denial.

Entitlement can go hand in hand with detrimental denial. I have seen this in parents who are overly image conscious and reject, outright, any suggestion that their kid may not be perfect. A mother I worked with who was a successful health care consultant could not bring herself to believe that her son had stolen a laptop computer from his school. Another parent, Rhea, petitioned her son Alex's private school for smaller homework assignments, although Alex did not have any special needs. This did not go over well with the school administration. Not surprisingly, Rhea eventually put Alex in another school, which Rhea later found fault with as well.

Entitlement can sometimes be more manipulative and subtle. This may take the form of an initial apology, followed by a "but" and then blame. For example, "I'm sorry Allison got upset with your daughter, but if your daughter had not provoked her, this situation would not have gotten to this point."

Rescuing children from natural consequences deprives them of any opportunity to learn responsibility for their actions. Appropriate advocating for your child's needs is far different from interfering with the life lessons your child may need to learn. Children suffer when they don't have to face the reality of their negative choices. Parents in detrimental denial run the risk of interfering with their children's abilities to problem solve and develop crucial coping skills.

Flaring-Up Toxic Thoughts

6. Emotional Overheating

Fifteen-year-old Amy had a hard time waking up for school. Bleary-eyed and in a rush one morning, she "borrowed" her mother's eyeliner. Tammy, Amy's mom, was under tremendous stress as a single parent also shouldering the care of her own very ill father. In addition, Tammy was anxiously waiting to see if she would survive a job layoff.

Finished with her makeup, Amy absentmindedly tossed the eyeliner for Tammy to catch, but Tammy was not looking. Struck in the head by the errant flying eyeliner, Tammy screamed at Amy and told her that she could no longer put up with her because she was an impossible daughter. Amy told me, "She's a freak. What did I do? It was an accident, and she is just acting psycho."

"Emotional overheating" occurs when a parent convinces herself that her child's behaviors can't be "handled." Emotional overheating involves a frantic need to escape or lash out on the part of the parent when she has difficulty relating to the child's emotions.

Many parents want to genuinely help their children but become frustrated when they themselves feel helpless. To be fair, feeling helpless, as a parent, is common. Specifically, we are conflicted between letting our children make mistakes and protecting them from disappointments.

Emotional overheating may also be turned inward and acted out passive-aggressively. Often, a parent acts this way because he perceives expressing emotions as a sign of weakness, which leads to emotional shutdown. Or the parent feels that ignoring his child is the most effective way to deal with negative thoughts and feelings.

By "shutting down," I mean not talking or slamming doors. We all know that children can also be masterful at this, particularly teens, but as adults parents are responsible for handling their emotions more effectively.

Emotional overheating is a major problem in parenting. Reacting impulsively and imposing rigid expectations and judgments sap the self-esteem of the child. The child's feelings and point of view are swallowed up or dismissed in the face of the parent's emotionality.

Claire was a mother I worked with who described her eleven-year-old son, Jonathan, as "very defiant." She told me, "I'm fast running out of patience. He is obsessed with video games and the computer. I limit how much he goes on a day, and I don't allow him to watch inappropriate shows or play violent games. His friends apparently get to watch and play whatever they want, whenever they want. My son has taken to telling me that I'm mean and he hates me and has started swearing at me. He gets extremely angry and unreasonable, and will not stop badgering me."

Claire came into my office one day after she grabbed him and pulled his hair. "I stopped myself but realized that my emotions were just boiling over." Once Claire learned about "emotional overheating," she then had to learn how to relax and become more mindful of all the thoughts in her head. Becoming mindful helps you learn how to "catch" your toxic thoughts as they occur. Claire was willing to address the problem and learned to replace her emotional-overheating tendencies with more adaptive patterns.

Occasionally, we hear stories about parents who suddenly discover that their children are in shocking, risky situations (acting out sexually or committing crimes). Flooding emotions are understandable in these situations. In most cases, however, parents who emotionally overheat are aware of what is going on in their child's life. Then the blowup usually comes from a gradual buildup of unmanageable stress and negative thoughts.

No parent is expected to be perfect. Emotional overheating needs to be discouraged, however, because these thoughts can easily tip over into verbal or physical abuse. Also, it often becomes a pattern, and the parent doesn't learn how to handle effectively her child's challenging behaviors. In reality, these behaviors are probably not as malicious as the parent assumes in the heat of the moment. The aftermath of emotional overheating, however, is that the child can lose respect for and also be fearful of the parent who blows up at him.

7. Blame Blasting

Regan instigated a fight with her younger brother, Javon. He then became angry at his sister Tamika, and he also became snippy with his mother, Sharon. Flooded with frustrations, Javon began to escalate his comments toward his mother. Sharon, very stressed from a difficult day at work, blamed Javon for ruining a calm dinner. She erroneously thought that her problems that night were all his fault.

Many children resent feeling blamed by their parents. Words and phrases such as "You made," "It's your," and "If only" are red flags in "blame blasting." You will know that you are blame blasting if you make statements like, "If only you would stop doing this, we'd be okay" or "If your lessons did not cost so much . . . " or "If you were a grateful kid, you would see . . . "

Blame is about denial. Detrimental denial, as I described earlier, is a dysfunctional attempt to protect children by refusing to see reality. Blame blasting, on the other hand, is a shaming devoid of empathy. Blaming your child for your discontent or your adult temper tantrums is downright cruel and unfair. Whether only thought or spoken out loud, blame blasting is damaging to children and the parent-child relationship. This can take the form of "You made me yell at you" or "You make me miserable" or, in more extreme cases, "You made me hit you!" Seemingly less aggressive but just as twisted is an initial apology followed by a "but": "I'm sorry I'm late, but if you were not so impossible getting ready for school this morning, then I would have had things planned out better."

A mother and son I worked with, Elaine and Trevor, painfully illustrate toxic blame. Elaine blamed Trevor for her financial stress because of his ADHD and the resultant counseling and tutoring he required. Elaine had a right to struggle with financial demands, but not to complain to him, as it caused him to "feel so stupid and worthless," in his own words.

When I asked Elaine, "How do you feel knowing Trevor feels useless?" she quickly said, "Oh, I don't want him to feel that way. I just want him to get on the ball and start taking care of himself more." I believed her when she said that she didn't intend to belittle him for his struggles. However, the outcome was that he *did* feel that way.

Parents get into blame because they are seeking an answer to the question, "Who did it?" rather than "What can we do about it?" Blame indicates a desire to punish. All this does is shut down the child. Blame leads to missed opportunities to resolve conflict, which leads to resentment, prolonging the incident and setting the stage for further clashes.

I am often asked, "But what if what I'm blaming her for *is* her fault?" I'm not saying responsibility is always fifty-fifty. Your child may have forgotten to do something, overlooked something, or gotten caught up in his own thing. But how you think and react is your responsibility, not his. If you stop focusing on who's to blame, then you can concentrate on the issue at hand, and *issues* are much easier to work through than *blame*.

8. "Should" Slamming

Trent and Jane, the parents of a twelve-year-old, Vicky, upon learning that she wanted to take a break from gymnastics, were concerned that she would throw away her talents. Vicky, who placed third in her state last year, felt that her parents were pressuring her. She and her parents argued about what she should do and think.

In his books *Ten Days to Self-Esteem* and *Feeling Good*, David Burns discusses what he terms the "shouldy" approach to life. He says that "should statements" directed against yourself lead to guilt and frustration. He explains that many people try to motivate themselves with *shoulds* and *shouldn't*s, as if they were delinquents who have to be punished before they can be expected to do anything. This usually doesn't work because all these *shoulds* and *musts* make you feel rebellious, and you get the urge to do just the opposite. Dr. Albert Ellis, another pioneer of cognitive therapy, had the concept of "musterbation," by which he means that we don't get upset by what the world does to us, we get upset by our false beliefs. Our expectations for our kids are full of *shoulds* and *musts*. But at the end of the day, we can only guide them to success; we can't force it on them.

"Should" statements, in general, lead to anger and frustration. "Musts," "oughts," and "have tos" are similar offenders. These kinds of absolute statements lead a child to feel guilty if he makes mistakes or struggles.

My friend and colleague Dr. James Karustis refers to thinking this way as being on "Planet Should." Dr. Karustis describes Planet Should as the world where things are the way they are supposed to be, where people always act decently and reasonably, and where parents never need to say, "I shouldn't have to tell you that again!"

Bruce was a frustrated father who sent his obstreperous thirteen-year-old son, Brock, to military school because Bruce felt Brock should learn structure and responsibility. As it turned out, Brock went AWOL from the school and failed to live up to his father's unrealistic expectations.

Too often when children fall short of our expectations, parents go "toxic" with "should" thoughts. These are particularly detrimental because they restrict the child's ability to think freely and learn for himself. This cripples the child's capacity to solve his own problems and grow.

When parents act like puppeteers, pulling on their kids' strings to make them something they are not, anger and frustration result for both sides. Toxic *shoulds* come from a sense of expectation, often rooted in our own childhoods and past relationships. For example, a mother who was told all her life by her parents to "figure out problems on her own" may rigidly feel that her daughter *should* learn more by her mistakes than through guidance. We often unknowingly bring these types of expectations into parenting.

A father I worked with felt his son should want to study law and join the family-owned law firm. Whereas the older brother happily followed this lucrative path, it was not for the younger one. Fortunately, Dad worked through his well-meaning yet overzealous expectations of his son and saw the light. He then chose to let go of what he felt his son "should do." This father instead did his son a big favor and got on board with his son's desire to become an auto technician. As father and son negotiated through their differing expectations, they reached a new mutual respect as well as gained a closer relationship.

Mary and her sixteen-year-old girl, Jody, came to see me after Jody blew up upon hearing one too many *should*s from her parents about her peer group. Mary felt that Jody *should* have different friends. Mary also believed that Jody should want to study more and strive to do better at school. Jody's outburst that particular day was not acceptable. At the same time, her parents' barrage of *should*s fueled her already poor impulse control. Jody did not have the emotional maturity to see her mother's concerns and fears and instead perceived her mother only as being unfair.

Like all toxic thoughts, *should*s often occur outside of our immediate awareness. Yet they are there—often as a result of our unrealistic, demanding need that our children meet our expectations rather than their own.

*Should*s are thoughts that are rigidly tied to standards. Good values and standards are important for healthy parenting. But rigid *should*s lead you to unfairly overlook the unique desires, strengths, and good intentions of your child. *Should*s slam the door shut on being able to understand where your child is truly coming from and what he is struggling with.

9. Dooming Conclusions

Christine was furious with her seven-year-old son, George. He was get-
ting in trouble in second grade with peers, and Christine was at her
wit's end. She'd begun to have dooming fantasies about George's be-
ing unable to get along with peers and make it in any school setting.
"I can only imagine how much worse this will get down the road." Any
two toxic-thinking patterns can merge together. In Christine's case, her
"should" thoughts joined with the "always or never" trap as she found
herself thinking, "Why does he always have to be the troublemaker at
school? I have given him great opportunities. But he is always mak-
ing things difficult."

Christine was caught up in "dooming conclusions." This is a
toxic-thinking pattern in which parents exaggerate the negative actions of and events concerning their children. A refusal to eat a
meal is distorted into an emerging eating disorder. A child struggles with a temporary fear of the dark, and the parent thinks, "She'll
never get over this." A week of grumpiness gets blown into "This
kid will bring down this whole family." Said another way, dooming
conclusions are highly negative, exaggerated predictions. These fatalistic thoughts block parents and children from working out problems together.

One of the ironies of dooming conclusions is that they can lead
not only to a breakdown of trust and communication but also to the
very event feared by the parent. Al, for example, became alarmed
as his fourteen-year-old son, Sean, spent increasing time on the
computer when he was supposed to be doing his homework. Al
convinced himself that Sean would end up failing his school year,
and, lo and behold, this became a reality. Fortunately, Sean and
his parents came in for counseling and came up with new time
boundaries that allowed for both work and play.

Stressed-out parents disappointed with their children's circumstances and achievements are at risk of dooming conclusions.
These projections can permeate any area of the child's life, including school ("He's going to fail out and be on the streets"), peers

("She will never make any friends), or home ("I can't ever see us having sanity in this house because of her antics").

Parents who have unresolved "emotional ghosts" from their pasts are particularly at risk for dooming conclusions. One woman I worked with feared that her angry seven-year-old son was going to end up like his maternal uncle, who was arrested for aggravated assault. Once I helped her differentiate her son's qualities from those of her brother, she was able to lighten up.

We all have some emotional ghosts from our pasts. I know a few people who had charmed childhoods; for most of us, life has both ups and downs. Yet some parents struggle more than others with childhood difficulties. I have seen parents struggle with the aftereffects of emotional or physical abandonment, addictions, financial stress, family mental illness, body-image problems, peer difficulties, learning disabilities, and many other types of issues. These concerns, and the lingering anxieties around them, if not worked through, can lead adults to fall into toxic-thought patterns with their own children.

Even just growing up with a pessimistic or negative parent can influence you to jump to negative conclusions with your own kids. Please be reassured, however, that even if your childhood was troubled in any way, this does not have to be your child's destiny, too. No matter what emotional baggage you have from your upbringing, there is always hope.

One very wealthy father with whom I worked, Joe, often exploded in anger with his two young children when they forgot to turn off light switches. He had grown up poor and with an often unemployed father. Joe feared that his own children would grow up not being aware of the value of a dollar. Joe got lost in thinking, "They will never appreciate how hard it is to make money, and they will drain me." Fortunately, Joe was willing to look at the differences between his life and his children's. He put things in a different perspective and worked through his skewed thoughts.

I also recall a mother who was ostracized by her field hockey teammates in seventh grade. When her ten-year-old daughter was teased in soccer, she became hypervigilant. She immediately assumed that her daughter would not learn how to fend for herself. Once the mother got her own emotional ghosts out of the way, she stopped overreacting and projecting her own unfounded fears onto her daughter.

Children rise to parental expectations. Healthy expectations encourage children to strive to be the best that they can be. Dooming conclusions, however, lead parents to dramatically lower their expectations or even give up on their kids. Dooming conclusions also create emotional chaos by short-circuiting kids' problem-solving skills and sense of personal empowerment.

As You Think Further About Toxic Thoughts . . .

While reading about the nine toxic-thought patterns that create tensions in parents' minds, you may have had one of those "Aha!" moments when you suddenly see your thought process being described. That's very common. But you may need more time to understand which pattern or patterns you need help with. You may need to "catch" yourself in a toxic moment. You may need to review these toxic patterns over the course of the next week or two.

The upcoming chapters focus on strategies for comforting your mind, tuning in, and talking back to your toxic thoughts. These toxic thoughts can easily be disputed and dealt with, as you'll soon see. You will be revisiting some of the examples in this chapter as you learn in detail how to detoxify in Chapters 6 and 7. Rest assured, there is hope—and you don't have to go to a family or child therapist to get it (unless, of course, you choose to). Keep on reading, and you will win the fight.

To Sum It All Up

By reading this chapter and getting to this point, you have
shown great courage and have made huge strides in gaining
self- and parenting awareness. Having learned about the
nine specific toxic-thought patterns, you no longer need to
feel in the dark about why you get worked up and frustrated
with your child. As you read further, try to reflect on the following key points:

- Having toxic thoughts does not make you a bad parent.
  Most parents struggle with toxic thoughts, and their sense
  of embarrassment and shame about having them leaves
  these thoughts denied and not dealt with.
- Toxic thoughts are distortions that sabotage your ability to understand, connect with, and problem solve with your
  children.
- You really do have control over how you think. When you
  consider and apply this crucial reality to how you view your
  children, the implications are huge for how they will, in turn,
  view themselves and respond to you.
- By learning about these nine toxic thoughts, you have already made significant progress in liking the child you
  love and reducing your PFS. No longer will you need to
  question *why* you get frustrated or wonder what you are
  really thinking in the midst of parenting stress.

Chapter 4

Kicking the
Parenting-Stress Habit

DIANA, A MOM OF TWO, one day complained, "There's just no end to it. I feel like my kids and husband drain everything out of me." Jeremy, a stay-at-home dad, vented similar concerns: "Some days I feel like my head is going to explode if I have to pick up one more thing that [two-year-old] Christian throws on the floor. Then, when the older ones come home from school and dump their stuff all over, I just want to howl at the sky."

Diana's and Jeremy's collective words are echoed inside the minds of countless other parents. Have you ever railed against how stressed out you get over your kids and wished that you could be calmer?

No matter your situation as a parent—a stay-at-home mom or a working dad, a single parent or a married one, a parent of one child or several—this chapter will be of great benefit to you. I am going to show you how to calm yourself down—even when your parenting stress feels like it is going to blast through the roof. If you follow this advice, you will dramatically lower your stress level, as learning to quiet your mind goes hand in hand with identifying, getting a grip on, and zapping those toxic thoughts.

Lowering your stress will also help you bypass your own emotional reactivity and find your emotional center, which will benefit

you as well as your kids. Think about it: No adult has ever complained to me that their own parents were too calm and understanding, or too good at keeping their cool. So let me show you
how to stick it to stress rather than letting stress stick it to you. I
tell my clients that life comes down to two important coping strategies: self-soothing and problem solving. Self-soothing is the ability
to calm down, and problem solving begins with the ability to think
rationally, as opposed to toxically.

Once you learn how to comfort your mind, then you can effectively open it up in order to learn the techniques I will explain in
Chapter 5. I will show you how to tune in to, and become more
aware of, toxic thoughts. In Chapters 6 and 7, you will learn alternative ways to think and react.

The first step in controlling toxic thoughts, however, is learning
how to calm down. We often tell our children to think before they
act. I am telling you that your parenting experiences will be so
much more satisfying once *you* learn to relax, to pause and be
mindful before you think or react. Learning to relax and become
more self-aware as a parent will make a huge difference in your
stress levels. I am going to share with you some very helpful relaxation strategies and exercises. First, let's take a look at what parenting stress really is and where it comes from.

Stress Is an Overwhelming Topic

Before learning how to lower your stress levels, it is important for
you to fully understand what I mean when I use the term. Seemingly countless definitions and experts have attempted to describe
stress. At the time of writing this chapter, I ran an Internet search
on the topic, and produced more 173 million hits. Wow! Clearly,
this is a popular search, so there must be some confusion about the
concept. No matter what definition you come across, however,
stress is nearly always seen as undesirable. When I use the term
stress, I will be referring to a state of emotional discomfort that re-

sults from feeling overwhelmed. This chapter explains all you need to know about stress and how to manage it.

Help, I'm Feeling Out of Control!

A more hands-on, helpful way to think about stress is as a psychological and physiological response to events that upset our personal balance in some way. When you feel out of balance, you feel out of control. That equals big-time stress!

Believe it or not, the feeling of stress you experience is meant to protect and support you. It is caused by our bodies' response system developed for our Stone Age ancestors to help them survive life-or-death situations like the attack of a hungry saber-toothed tiger. Of course, in modern times, we do not frequently come across saber-toothed tigers. Then again, when your child is acting impossible, you may feel you stand a better chance of taming a tiger than your kid.

When we face a perceived threat, whether to our physical safety or emotional equilibrium, our bodies' defenses kick into high gear. This is a rapid, automatic process known as the "fight-or-flight" response. We all know what this feels like: heart pounding in the chest, muscles tensing up, breath coming faster, and every one of our senses on red alert. People who have panic attacks experience this response intensely, out of proportion to the triggering event.

Check out "A Closer Look at Your Body's Stress Response" to get a more detailed sense of what goes on in your body when you feel high levels of stress. As you will see, getting stressed out involves some complex mechanisms.

A Closer Look at Your Body's Stress Response

The "fight-or-flight" response involves a chain of biological changes that prepare us for emergency action. When your brain senses danger, your sympathetic nervous system responds by releasing a flood of stress hormones, including adrenaline, norepinephrine, and cortisol. These stress hormones race through the bloodstream, readying you to either flee the scene or battle it out.

Your heart rate and blood flow to your large muscles increase so you can run faster and fight harder. Blood vessels under your skin constrict to prevent blood loss in case of injury, your pupils dilate so you can see better, and your blood sugar ramps up, giving you an energy boost and speeding up reaction time. At the same time, any bodily processes that are not essential to immediate survival are suppressed. The digestive and reproductive systems slow down, growth hormones are switched off, and the immune response is inhibited.

● ●

Parenting Stress Is Inescapable

When your child acts up, he certainly (thank goodness!) is not a threat to you in the same way as a dangerous wild animal. Nonetheless, your primitive stress response gets activated because you feel out of control. Aren't kids masterful at knocking us off our emotional balance? Like when your young child asks you the same question three hundred times in a row? Or when your middle school child feels that it is his job to relentlessly pick on his younger sibling to toughen him up? Or how about when your high schooler was supposed to be home from that party an hour and a half ago, and still has not contacted you? First, you pray for his safety, then you tell yourself that once he's safe you're going to let him have it like never before.

A client of mine once described parenting as waking up and finding herself standing on the top of a cliff with her arms spread while praying that a big wind did not blow her over the edge. Talk about a powerful visual! Even if your stress doesn't feel that dramatic, that feeling of being overwhelmed hits most parents all too often.

Putting it plainly and simply, parenting stress largely comes from wanting to control what we *can't* control. We are never going to be able to dictate our children's behaviors or all the elements of their lives to the degree we would like. Seeing your child make mistakes and often learn things the hard way is enough to make you tear your hair out.

The Hidden Cause of Your Stress

So who causes you to feel stress when your kids do things that upset you? Who makes you feel like you want to pull your own hair out? You may think that the obvious answer is your child who creates those irritating conflicts. Wrong! You see, the actual person causing you to get upset . . . is you. Hold on, I'm a parent, too. And it certainly used to feel to me like my kids caused me to get upset with them. But that is simply not true for me, and it is not true for you.

It feels quite satisfying to blame your kids for *making* you feel upset. It allows us to avoid taking responsibility for our own thoughts and feelings. But as adults, we need to lose the "victim to circumstances" mentality and get real. The truth is that it is how you interpret your child's behavior that causes you to become upset. Your child is not the one who tells you what to feel or how to react. That comes from your own mind.

If it is not easy for you to accept that you create your own parenting stress, then think back to the nine toxic thoughts from the previous chapter. Those unhealthy thinking patterns are what *truly* get you upset and stressed out. And once you learn to think in a less destructive and more flexible way, you are on the way to lower stress and PFS levels. By learning how to comfort yourself through stress reduction, you will have a much easier time listening in for those toxic thoughts and zapping them.

Stressed-Out Parents Stress Their Children

A major problem with letting stress rule you is that it also strains your children. When you let the pressure get to you, your child may react in several possible ways: He can be avoidant, sad, frustrated, confused, or angry. Keep in mind that he probably does not have the self-awareness and coping skills to take your stress in stride.

Often in my practice I see teary-eyed teens who have made some bad choices. I also see their anxious parents pleading with them to be honest so they can understand why the difficulties arose. The problem is that when parents are frequently tense, their children become unwilling to share their thoughts and feelings. They fear it can lead only to yelling or being in more trouble.

Just as I was writing this chapter, one of my own children let me know that I had unwittingly slipped into lecture mode. I was not listening as well as I could have. I had been worried and thought that lectures would help. But I soon realized that my lectures actually were manifestations of my own toxic thoughts and stress. Once I started accepting that imposing my solutions was not the solution, I shifted gears. I told her that I was going to shut my mouth, open my ears, and just listen to her. We sat silently together for about five minutes (which felt like five hours to me). As I focused myself on being less demanding and less aggressive, I also felt less stressed out. My daughter then started opening up to me about some of her own concerns. Go figure!

Whether your stress leads you to lecture, whine, scream, clam up, or be crabby, it keeps you from being an effective parent. Managing your stress and tuning in to your toxic thoughts keeps the doors of communication open between you and your child. And the more you communicate, the more you will like each other. But unless you are first open with yourself about how you handle your stress, it will be hard to make positive changes to your patterns of communication with your child.

Many of us hold on to the myth that families are (or should be) free from stress, that the home should be a constant haven of peace and tranquillity. We live for those joyful moments that take our breath away. But sometimes, trying to balance everything that life throws at you makes you feel like it is hard to breathe. The good news is that you really can manage stress, especially once you acknowledge it and resolve to deal with it.

Recent research has shown that stressed-out parents can weaken their *children's* immune systems. This illustrates how tightly interwoven the emotions of parents and children really are. I have seen firsthand well over a thousand children in my practice who have benefited when their parents learned to manage their own stress more effectively.

Lowering your own stress will allow you to control your toxic thoughts. Managing your worries in positive ways will also teach valuable lessons to your kids. Many adults in my practice share how their own parents did not cope well with anxiety. Unlearning these unhealthy patterns can be difficult, but the reward is a smoother and more joyous relationship with your child. You also will be a valuable role model to your child.

Your Stress Is Not Only Parental

You most likely have worries that come from people and situations other than your kids. Marital hassles or divorce, keeping your boss happy, financial pressures, and dealing with your family of origin can all prove challenging, to say the least. Let's take a quick look at some of these other stressors that parents have to deal with. The information and strategies in this chapter can help with each of them.

Marital or Couple Stress

A fulfilling marriage is a wonderful asset to have in this challenging world. All husbands and wives and other intimate partners, however, face challenges. It is not easy to keep love alive and thriving, especially when you are also parents. Taking one another for granted and having unrealistic expectations lead to most difficulties that couples face.

It is important that relationship stress is managed because (as with other stressors) avoiding these issues usually makes them worse. Couples coming to see me in the eleventh and a half hour have a much harder time saving their marriage compared to couples who work proactively to keep their relationship healthy. Poor marriages are detrimental to children just as much as parents. One of the best gifts that couples can give to their kids is to take care of their relationship.

Divorce Stress

A client of mine once described how in the aftermath of his divorce, he felt as if he had thrown a rock in a pond and then saw the ripples spread much farther than he expected. I experienced a similar sensation after my own divorce and believe it is a common one. I have a solid coparenting relationship with the mother of my children; time, mutual effort, and counseling can heal old wounds for many families. For other children and parents, however, divorce can be like a cancer. It can eat away at goodwill and cooperation when all parties are trying to move forward. Being a single parent and shouldering the demands of a difficult divorce can be very stressful—both on the parents and on the children.

Work Stress

A significant cause of stress is work. Demanding bosses, competitive co-workers, and difficult clients can quickly lead you to perceive your job as a place of misery. However, it is not only the routine tasks and pressures of work that can lead to stress. In fact, worrying about holding on to a job in today's competitive world is stressful. Unfortunately, the strain of both work itself and the possibility of unemployment creates a cycle in which people feel they have to work even harder in order to keep their jobs, only feeding anxieties.

Financial Pressures

Money is another major cause of stress for parents. Most parents feel that there never seems to be enough of it. The pressures of mortgages or rents, car payments, credit cards, and other bills can wreak havoc on the emotional balance of parents struggling to make ends meet. For many couples, money stress keeps piling up higher and higher, and there never seems to be a way out. Living within one's means and getting solid advice from a trusted financial adviser are important steps to take to reach more financial stability and reduce your anxieties.

Extended-Family Issues

As adults, we have the benefits of maturity over our children but can be dragged down by the baggage from the families in which we were raised. Problems may arise when parents in the "sandwich generation" struggle to meet the demands of their children while also dealing with the demands of their aging parents. In many cases, there are also tensions between spouses and in-laws. These conflicts can lead to torn loyalties to the spouse versus members of the family of origin. If not handled with wisdom and perspective, these difficulties will add to your problems with your children.

SOS for Managing Stress: Seventeen Proven Parenting-Stress Reducers

Now that I have covered what stress is and where it comes from, it is time for you to learn ways to reduce it. The strategies that follow are by no means exhaustive, but I believe that they are very helpful for the all the stresses faced by parents like you.

You will find your child much more likable if you are not so stressed out. And the less stressed you are, the more you will also like yourself as a parent. By lowering your anxiety and worry, you will be less prone to toxic thoughts, and you'll be much more able to tune in and overcome them. Managing strain in positive ways will also teach valuable lessons to your children. Many adults have shared with me that having grown up with anxious parents was very hard, because they were never shown effective tools for dealing with the demands of life.

To learn how to lower your stress, you need to replace your unhealthy coping mechanisms with more positive ones. And even if you were lucky and had outstanding models for handling stress, it never hurts to bone up on the most effective strategies. So to help you in this regard, below are seventeen time-tested strategies that will help you lower anxiety, relax your mind, and prepare you to manage your toxic thoughts.

1. Breathe Your Way to a Clear Mind

Breathing is an excellent way to slow down and become more conscious of what goes on in your mind. It lowers stress because it slows racing thoughts and feelings.

You may be initially skeptical about this "mindfulness" stuff. Maybe you are asking what it has to do with toxic thinking and getting your kid to stop being such a pain in the backside. Let me say that once you experience mindfulness, I think the clarity it provides will be very apparent. The less stressed out you are, the more your child will follow your lead and be less stressed, too. You will be pleasantly surprised.

As you will see in "Breathing Your Way to Mindful Parenting," the easiest way to become mindful is to learn how to breathe with awareness. When you catch yourself having a toxic thought, make a point to BREATHE deeply. Yes, it's simple. But simple is good. Deep breaths will calm and slow you down. The next time you're upset or angry, notice your breath. You're probably going to find it stuck in your chest or throat. Our natural inclination is to stop breathing or breathe extremely shallowly when stressed. But it's hard to remain clenched and toxic when you have breath flowing through your body. Dr. Andrew Weil, the famous Harvard-trained physician, views breathing as "the master key to self-healing."

I recall Troy, a former professional football player and dad of one of my preteen clients. Troy would erupt in anger over little things, which was hard for his son—and also did not do wonders for Troy's marriage. When I asked Troy if he'd be willing to do some deep-breathing work to mindfully reduce his stress and anger, he initially looked at me like I was a tackling dummy. I am pleased to share, however, that Troy was soon thrilled by how much he could reduce his stress, PFS, and anger through deep breathing. Suffice it to say, his wife was also most grateful.

Breathing Your Way to Mindful Parenting

It is important to note that most people habitually breathe short, shallow breaths, which leads to retaining stale air, incomplete oxidation of the tissues, and muscle tension. So realize that you get a two-for-one deal: You are breathing for both mindfulness and physical health. Mindful breathing is shown in the steps below.

- Breathe in deeply through your nose to a count of four.
- Picture your breath in your mind as it slowly goes in your nose, down your throat and windpipe, and into your stomach.
- As you breathe in, allow your stomach and your chest to expand with air.

- Hold this breath for a count of four.
- Exhale slowly to a count of seven or eight, watching your breath in your mind as it goes the reverse route and out your mouth (to get even more out of this, say the word *calm* to yourself as you breathe out).
- Repeat at least three times, or until you feel calm.

2. Parent the Young Dude (or Dudette) with Gratitude

I am sure you wish things could be easier. Does it seem like every other parent has an unfair advantage? Maybe your neighbor has parents who come by and do the laundry or help out. Perhaps you know other parents who have trust funds. Maybe you think an only child would be easier than your brood of three kids.

No doubt about it. Life is not easy when you are a parent, and it certainly can seem like your life is unduly demanding compared to others'. Yet a lot of your stress comes from desiring things to be different. And guess what? Wishing life were easier can make it more miserable than it has to be.

Become proficient at counting your blessings. The more you do, the less stress you'll feel. In my years of being a psychologist I have heard and seen many tragic stories, including illnesses, accidental deaths, suicides, relentless addictions, and more. So keep your problems in perspective: Your child's complaints about his new sneakers not being "cool" enough pale in comparison to having a child who can't walk.

Perhaps you are thinking, "Okay, Dr. Jeff, this gratitude stuff makes sense, but does it *really* work?" Or you may think it works, but only momentarily. You may have a point. We all have our down days, gratitude or no. But I am reminding you to celebrate what you have rather than dwell on what you don't have, or even *wish* you had. Liking your child gets easier when you embrace that he is alive and, one hopes, healthy, and that he is a gift.

If you realize that things are going wrong and your planned Kodak moment falls apart, then I suggest that you use the change of plans as a time to reflect. It has been said that for every one thing that goes wrong, there are probably ten or fifty or one hundred blessings. Look for them, and you will feel less stressed out.

3. Give Yourself the Power of Positive Energy

I have found that the first thoughts on my mind when I wake up have a major influence on the tone of my day. I encourage you to start each morning doing something to create a positive mind-set. If you are into prayer or formal religion, then call on your faith. Maybe watering your flowers perks you up. Or perhaps jumping on that piece of exercise equipment gets you going in a positive direction and gives you peace of mind, too.

And it's not only important when waking up; looking for the positive is an ongoing process. Our daily lives frequently present us with challenges, and it is important to keep filling our tank all day long.

The world is your oyster, and positive energy abounds if you look for it. You probably have some ideas as to where you might find it. I suggest that every day, you take time to do something you really enjoy. I have provided a few ideas and left spaces for you to add to the list:

- Read something inspirational
- Watch a favorite movie
- Listen to music that makes you feel great
- Call up a friend you haven't talked to in some time
- Observe well-mannered young families and children and absorb their positive energy
- _____
- _____
- _____
- _____

In addition to building positive habits, it's important to avoid negative ones. Don't fall prey to toxic thoughts about yourself, such as "I'm too old to . . . " or "I'm too fat to . . . " and so on. As you may recall from Chapter 3, the word *should* creates a lot of pressure in our lives. Try to eradicate that word from your vocabulary as well as other energy-draining words such as *hate*. Believe that most people are doing the best they can. I also find it helpful to exercise, talk to friends, and think about things that excite me.

4. Ask Yourself, "What Is the Worst Thing That Can Happen?"

A lot of stress comes from worries that start with "What if?" The best antidote is to ask yourself, "What is the worst thing that can happen?" Realize what is worth getting worried about and what isn't. This is called choosing your battles wisely. One wonderful way of letting go of what you can't control is to say the serenity prayer:

God grant me the courage to change the things I can change,
The serenity to accept the things I can't change,
And the wisdom to know the difference.

5. Be Prepared

The Boy Scouts have a motto: Be prepared. Following the Scouting spirit, stay calm and collected by preparing in advance. Prep for morning madness by being proactive the evening before, like Pam, a divorced mother of four elementary-age children, who used that time to set the breakfast table, make lunches, and get her kids' books and supplies together. She found that the extra planning allowed her to thwart chaos before school.

Planning for success also means planning for mishaps. Remember that procrastination leads to more stress. Do today what you'd rather put off until tomorrow. Here are tips to on being prepared:

- Remember that you can still be nice even if you say no. I coached an overextended parent named Don to say no to extra projects, social activities, work committees, and invitations he simply did not have the time or energy for. This took some practice, but Don discovered that he could maintain the respect of others as he became more judicious in deciding where to put his time and energy.
- When possible, practice preventive maintenance for your car and appliances. Staying on top of maintenance schedules can help you avoid becoming bogged down with an untimely repair.
- Inoculate yourself against a feared event. For example, one of my adult clients, Kurt, found it helpful to prime himself before making a presentation to higher-ups at work. Kirk found it invaluable to take the time to go over every part of the experience in his mind. He imagined what he'd wear, what his audience would look like, how he would present his talk, what questions would be asked, and how he would answer them. Not surprisingly, he was told his talk was a "slam dunk" when he made the actual presentation.
- Organize your home and workspace so that you always know exactly where things are. Organizational skills are not my personal strong suit. To compensate, I have found that putting things away where they belong prevents the stress of losing things.
- Have duplicates of everything you can afford to, such as flashlights, cases for contact lenses, pencils (with erasers), keys, nail clippers, pens, and so forth.
- Don't let the gas tank get below one-quarter full. (By the way, if you happen to pass me on the road pulled over with an empty tank, please tell me that I told you to tell me so.)
- Don't wait until you're down to your last bus token or postage stamp to buy more.

- Don't put up with something that doesn't work right. If your alarm clock, wallet, shoelaces, windshield wipers, or whatever are a constant aggravation, get them fixed or get new ones. One of my clients, Shirley, a mom of triplets, called herself a professional pitcher for being able to pitch (toss out or donate) all unneeded items that caused clutter. She inspired me to do so as well.

6. Write It Down

Whether you use a handheld device or keep a good old-fashioned pad and pencil, write down appointment times, when to pick up the dry cleaning, when library books are due, and the like. As I was discussing this chapter with a friend, he shared with me an apt ancient Chinese proverb: "No memory is as firm as faded ink!"

7. Exercise

I can't emphasize enough the value of exercise. It has lifted my mood many times. There are many benefits of exercise, and the more established, well-known ones include:

- It reduces the risk of heart disease, high blood pressure, osteoporosis, diabetes, and obesity
- It keeps joints, tendons, and ligaments flexible, which makes it easier to move around
- It reduces some of the effects of aging
- It contributes to your mental well-being and helps treat depression
- It helps relieve stress and anxiety
- It increases your energy and endurance
- It helps you sleep better
- It helps you maintain a normal weight by increasing your metabolism (the rate at which you burn calories)

8. Don't Believe in Wasted Time

Only our perception of time creates a sense of time pressure. Most of us spend far too much time worrying about the limited amount of time we have when we can be enjoying the precious present moments. Years ago I spent a week at a monastery of Buddhist monk Thich Nhat Hahn, where I learned many valuable lessons. He suggests, for example, that the next time you're stuck at a red light, don't sweat it. Rather, remain calm, pay attention to your breathing, and smile while thinking or even saying aloud, "Breathing in, I calm my body. Breathing out, I smile." The red light then "becomes a friend, helping us remember it is only in the present moment that we can live our lives."

Managing time comes from managing your expectations around it. Be prepared to wait. A paperback or magazine can make the doctor's office or post office almost pleasant. Keep the following in mind, and you'll feel better about time in no time:

- Accept that there will always be projects in progress.
- Periodically reexamine your standards for housekeeping.
- Purchase goods and services that buy you time, such as a lawn mowing service if you can afford it.
- Let go of the "superparent" myth. Relax your standards. The world will not end if all the mulch does not get put down this weekend.
- Give yourself credit for tasks accomplished, even for a small piece of a project.
- Select commitments very carefully.
- Limit time spent on the telephone.

9. You "Really Need" What?

You don't want your child to impulsively cross a busy road or accidentally step on broken glass. These are times you *need* your child to listen to you. But beyond staying safe and other basic physical needs (food, water, shelter), remember that most things we want for children are only preferences. The less you get attached to your preferences, the less they will become sources of stress.

Celine, a mother in my practice, preferred that her daughter work up to her potential in school. You may say, of course, that makes sense. What parents in their right minds would not prefer that their children do well in school? What stressed Celine out, however, were her persistent attempts to convince her overly social daughter to change her study habits.

Our kids tend to see these types of "needs" as controlling. Teenagers, in particular, are more likely to rebel when they feel pressured into things. The best way to avoid these power struggles is to remember that your desires really are preferences. Keep expectations of achievement in school at a reasonable level; encourage your children to strive for things and attempt challenging work, but don't push them into situations that are too difficult or may negatively impact their self-esteem. In the end, they will learn from their own mistakes better than from your protection. Celine's daughter, Tina, shared with me that she wanted to study more when her mother nagged her less.

10. Be Flexible in Your Outlook

Rigid views increase stress. Life is full of challenges, but developing a flexible attitude will go a long way toward adjusting to the inevitable ups and downs. There is a lot to say for learning to "go with the flow," as life seldom goes completely as planned and does not come with guarantees. Job losses, child struggles, health concerns, and the deaths of loved ones are all part and parcel of life. Here are some tips for flexibility when life does not go the way you would like it to:

- *Get out of your comfort zone and embrace change.* Change is necessary to get anywhere in life, and embracing it takes a lot of courage and strength. After all, change brings us into new experiences, and often the unknown is scary. Change also brings a good omen, in that life is not remaining stagnant but, rather, is moving forward in different directions. We are better off allowing life to carry us in these directions so we can experience a different point of view and gain a better appreciation of what we do or don't have.
- *Enjoy the journey.* Being goal oriented is great, but enjoying the ride along the way is even better. If you constantly focus on doing something, achieving something, or acquiring something, you may lose sight of yourself and who you really are. So remember to enjoy yourself and those you love along the way.
- *Don't take it all so personally.* I think we take life way too seriously. Yes, it is easy to become frustrated at times, but emotionally detaching when you do will allow you to stop overreacting. This will help you look at your options more carefully and objectively.
- *Envision a new outcome.* If we go through life expecting things to go as they always have, we can never open ourselves up to the possibility of great things. When our expectations are not met, we will be lost, not knowing which way to turn. If we can imagine our actions having different outcomes, we can be prepared for whatever life may bring us, good or bad. You get to choose the conclusion of your daily challenges. Being calm, firm, understanding, and noncontrolling in conflicts with your child will nip nasty arguments before they begin.

11. Get Enough Sleep

A good night's sleep allows you to tackle the day's stress better. When you are tired, you are less patient and easily agitated. Most adults need seven to eight hours of sleep per night. Practicing good sleep habits along with stress-lowering tactics can help improve your quality of sleep. In periods of stress, allowing a wind-down time in the evening can be very helpful. You might try:

- using a diary to make a list of things you have to deal with
- taking a warm bath
- taking slow, relaxing deep breaths
- praying
- imagining yourself lying on a soft, white, puffy cloud
- doing some yoga or stretches

But don't go to sleep quite yet—you are almost done with this chapter.

12. Write About It

I wrote earlier about the importance of writing down logistical demands to keep things straight and keep your stress level low. In the same way that exercise can reduce your stress, writing about what is on your mind helps a lot, too. I have kept a journal since 1993. I started writing daily and then slacked off. I mentioned to a friend that I could not keep the journal I had started, as I found it difficult to write entries every day. My friend then wisely suggested I remove the sense of obligation and just write in it whenever I want.

I am proud to say I still keep my journal. Some years there have been more than one hundred entries and some just a couple. The bottom line is that there is a magic that occurs when you write down your thoughts and feelings (in a journal or on a paper to be thrown away). It gives you clarification and a renewed perspective. Sometimes the entries in my journal are of a venting nature, and sometimes they are more positive. The wonderful thing is that your journal can be anything you want it to be. Be sure to keep it in a private place, and be cautious of what you write in case anyone ever comes across it, especially your children.

13. Talk It Out

Troubled people often feel that they have no one to talk to. Discussing your problems with a trusted friend or, if needed, a mental health professional can help clear your mind so you can concentrate on problem solving. As a psychologist, I have seen over and over again how good people feel when they are understood.

14. Talking Less Is Good, Too

When interacting with others, particularly your children, it is often best to talk less and listen more. Recently, Dennis, the father of Scott, said something very powerful to me: "You know, Dr. Jeff, I now realize that my job is to guide Scott instead of imposing my expectations on him all the time." I smiled and told Dennis how gratifying it was to hear how he "got it." The more you listen, the more your kids will talk about what bothers them. The more you lecture them, the more they will shut down. The more your kids share with you, the less stressed out you will be at having to wonder what is going on inside their heads.

15. Do for Others

The more we help out others, the more we help ourselves feel better, too. Make a meal for someone who is in need. Hold a door open. Smile at someone. Focus on understanding rather than on being understood, on loving rather than on being loved. Many philosophers and scholars, including the Dalai Lama, talk about the merits of making yourself happy by trying to give happiness to others.

16. Take a Time-Out

A twelve-year-old client gave me the following advice for parents who "spaz out": "When you get angry with your child, don't yell or scream. Instead, go to your room, lock your door, and think before you act."

Deidra, a mother of three young children, would put herself in time-out when she was losing it with one of her kids. I encouraged her to remember when she was feeling at the end of her emotional rope how she wanted this child before she was born, how innocent she was, and how much she loved her. Deidra put this coping strategy into action when her daughter hurled a serving spoon with gravy across the kitchen. Putting herself in time-out helped prevent her from screaming with frustration.

17. Get Away Any Way You Can

Weeklong family vacations are great, but sometimes you need a break more often than once or twice a year. A morning out for bagels breaks up the daily routine. Miniature golf is fun, and a driving range is a great place to let go of PFS tensions, too.

Plan miniretreats that give you a break from your routine and allow downtime when you can just hang out. See if a local hotel with a swimming pool has off-season rates. You can also turn off the TV, telephone, and computer for the night, cook an easy meal or order takeout, tell stories, or play cards or a board game. Teenagers may think it's weird at first, but they really do appreciate the change of pace and the time with their family.

Develop family traditions with your immediate and extended family members. Come up with a special night once or twice a year that isn't tied to a holiday. Have everyone who comes make something to eat. Share what you have been doing since the last get-together, and come up with some fun game that everyone can get involved in. Horseshoes, softball, badminton—all are fine. The game isn't important. Rather, it's the time you spend together goofing around without judgment and the pressures of the regular schedule of life.

To Sum It All Up

By reading so far, you're already well on your way to becoming less stressed. As you continue on, please keep the following points in mind about managing your parenting stress:

- Stress is very real for parents and needs to be managed.
- Stress comes from feeling emotionally off balance and out of control.
- The more you manage your stress, the more you will be able to manage your children.
- If you apply the strategies presented in this chapter, you will be well on your way to lowering your stress level.

Chapter 5

Becoming a
More Mindful Parent

MAYBE YOU ARE STILL SKEPTICAL that you are one of those parents with toxic thoughts. Do you ever find yourself in a situation with your child, surprised at your own reaction? Do you find yourself saying, "I don't know what I was thinking—I wanted to run away" or "I just blew up"? From now on, you won't have to wonder what you are thinking. This chapter offers powerful tools for becoming aware of your thoughts. No longer will the contents of your mind be elusive.

Thoughts drive behaviors. And this is not just the case in parenting. It is true in all parts of life. A major league baseball player who convinces himself that he will strike out runs a far greater risk of whiffing at the plate than one who does not. A salesperson who holds negative feelings toward a prospective client is going to have a hard time not letting those vibes get in the way of making the deal. And last, but certainly not least, a parent holding toxic thoughts about her child is going to be more prone to judging her child, yelling at him, and developing PFS.

In Chapter 3, I introduced the nine toxic thoughts of parenting. Then in Chapter 4, I helped you learn how to relax your mind. Learning how to relax and comfort yourself by using those strategies and tools is a big step forward in becoming a more mindful parent. In this chapter we are going to take a closer look at what "mindfulness" means and how it can help you identify your toxic thoughts as they occur.

The Effects of Mindfulness Are Invaluable

Mindfulness allows you to really pay attention to your toxic thoughts. It also allows you to react with more maturity toward your child. It will prevent you from becoming depressed and discouraged from the stress of parenting, or from becoming a short-fused overreactor. As you become more mindful, you will become more patient—with yourself and with your child.

Mindfulness allows you to work smarter, as opposed to harder. The journey of becoming more mindful never ends, especially when it comes to understanding our children. The more we can listen and understand them, and pay attention to our thoughts in the process, the more we will learn to accept their individuality and the decisions they make. We will finally be able to *support* them rather than unwittingly sabotage their best interests.

A Four-Step Plan to Tune in to Your Toxic Thoughts

The following four simple steps will take you far on your journey into parenting mindfulness. This will become very easy to do. All you need to do is read on with desire and an open mind.

Getting into the Thought-Finding Habit

Our minds are unique, and that's what makes us all individuals. No matter how much you pride yourself on being a unique individual, however, you also have something in common with me. You are a creature of habit. We are all creatures of habit. Although we are certainly not robots, for the most part we have set ways of thinking and doing things. In fact, from the time we wake up, most of what we do, eat, and think will be the same as it was yesterday.

We rely on habits, a.k.a. autopilot, for everything from getting to work to brushing our teeth to drinking coffee. Haven't you ever had those times of getting in the car, driving to work—and not really remembering driving there? There's no doubt about it: Habits come in handy and can be quite useful because they save time and give us rapid responses to all kinds of events, especially daily tasks. It would be overwhelming if we had to think through every decision as if for the first time. Can you list below the habits that have become helpful in your life?

_____

_____

_____

_____

_____

_____

We all have some habits we would like to change. Can you list below any of your habits you would like to change?

_____

_____

_____

_____

_____

_____

Thinking Patterns Are Habits Too

As you can see from doing the exercises above, some habits are healthy and work well for us. At the same time, other habits aren't so helpful. Take another look at the list of toxic thoughts on page xviii. Having these as habits of thinking won't make parenting too much fun.

So how do you get out of the toxic-thinking rut? Trying to create new thinking habits because we *should* is rarely effective. Instead, focus on your specific reasons for wanting to change these
toxic-thinking habits. This will empower you to make a real change
rather than putting pressure on yourself that will only backfire.

To bolster your willpower, write down your motivations for detoxifying your thoughts in the spaces below. Perhaps you want to reduce
conflict with your child, understand your child better, or have a more
open relationship. As your write in the spaces below, consider the following questions: How will thinking less toxically impact other areas of your life? How will it affect your spouse, children, job, income,
social contacts, and physical health? The more thorough you are
when doing this exercise, the more you will see the benefits and the
easier it will be for you to follow through. Keep writing until you
can't imagine a life without this new behavior.

In order to change your thinking habits, you need to become
clear on what you are thinking in the first place. This mindfulness
will pave the way to changing your thinking and emotional habits.
You are going to go from being a toxic-thought overreactor to a
toxic-thought zapper.

Remember to use the relaxation tools described in Chapter 4. Keep practicing those exercises and the exercises in the chapters that follow for a minimum of twenty-one days. Research shows that it takes at least three weeks to develop a new habit. Zig Ziglar, a noted self-help author and speaker, wisely says, "People often say that motivation doesn't last. Well, neither does bathing—that's why we recommend it daily." You may now be catching yourself thinking toxic thoughts all the time, but you will need a few weeks—*at least*—to train yourself to relax, focus, and change your toxic-thinking patterns. For most of your life, you haven't paid close attention to your idle self-talk. It can take time to create this new habit. Following is my four-step model for catching and stopping your toxic thoughts.

Step 1: Listen to Your Toxic Thoughts

My guess is that simply reading through the nine toxic thoughts has already gotten you thinking, "Aha, wow, I really think that!" It is my hope that as you have been reading this book, you've already begun to catch yourself. If this is the case, then this is fantastic. If you have not yet noticed those toxic thoughts, then maybe you need more time to tune in. That's fine too. Whether you want to get even better at becoming aware of your toxic thoughts or are still looking to discover them, then you will find the exercises in the pages that follow very helpful.

Many parents become habituated to reacting in certain ways to their children, and they do not recognize their toxic thoughts as they occur in "real time." I have heard many parents question how they are supposed to know what they are thinking when they are in the middle of a frustrating argument with their child.

In fact, most parents notice their own anger only once they are already yelling. Well, if so, at least you have begun to name your feelings. That shows you are paying attention to how you feel, which is a start and a step in the right direction. But let's go further so that you can gain more control of your thoughts and emotions. The next step is paying attention to what you think, and discovering which thoughts drive problematic feelings.

Elena, mother of Gwen, was quite skeptical of the benefits of mindfulness. Elena had initially told me, "Dr. Jeff, who on earth has got time and energy to listen to themselves? I certainly don't. My mind just goes all nuts and gets scrambled. Then I yell at Gwen—that's all there is to it." I then said, "Elena, you have already *not* been listening in for your toxic thoughts. And based on what you have been telling me, you are struggling with your frustration and anger with your daughter. I wonder if you can't hear your toxic thoughts right now because you're not trying. And from what you are telling me, Elena, these hidden thoughts are allowing your emotions to get the best of you." Elena replied bitingly, "Okay, so how am I supposed to hear what I am saying to myself about my impossible daughter?" I just smiled. "I just heard something that sounded toxic—did you?" Elena slumped down in her chair as she realized that she often labeled Gwen "impossible."

There are many parents like Elena who question if it is possible to become mindful of their toxic thoughts. Here's the good news: I know you can. I have worked with more than two thousand parents who have learned how and gained more control of their emotions. I know you can achieve this too if you work at it. Just let go of your doubts and simply listen in. The more you work at it, the more you start tuning in, the more you *will* become aware of them. You don't have to stand on your head, meditate, or go to a quiet room. All you really have to do is pay active attention to your internal thoughts, and what words come out of your mouth, especially when you realize you're thinking about your child. Naturally, the quality of your direct interactions with your child will reinforce what you think about him. So a good time to check in with your thoughts is when you're with your child, or immediately afterward.

As you become more mindful, you will discover that you can also tune in during those quiet times when you're in the shower, walking the dog, or commuting to work. Listen to what you're telling yourself. Remember, your mind is open twenty-four hours. Naturally, not all of your thoughts will be about your child, but if you are suffering from PFS, then you can bet a very good number of them are. Once Elena got more in touch with her toxic thoughts, she couldn't believe the buzzing in her head. "Dr. Jeff, there I was waiting in the parking lot at a soccer game, and I really had some big-time self-awareness. I even wrote down my thoughts like you suggested, just so I could see them. Though I knew I was upset with Gwen for refusing to do things I asked her to around the house, I didn't realize how much I was getting myself worked up. I was shocked at the amount of time I spent dwelling on how she is so lazy."

The good news is that you can always go back and rethink things. After an argument with your child, prompt yourself with questions like "What was I telling myself about the way Jacob was acting?" or "What was I thinking right before I screamed at Janis?"

I encourage you to be patient with yourself as you become more self-aware. Remember, don't feel that you *should* be able to immediately catch yourself. Rather, the goal is to eventually catch yourself thinking toxic thoughts about your child (it's not a contest; it's a process). The last thing I want you to do is label yourself incompetent for having difficulty getting rid of your toxic thoughts. How maddening and unproductive would that be? Trust me, the more that you work on it, the easier it will become.

Here are four tips for zooming in on toxic thoughts about your child:

1. *Listen for the language of toxic thinking.* As you now know, toxic thinking encourages the use of certain words and phrases, such as "always and never" (the "always or never" trap), "You're lazy" (label gluing), "Yeah, right, sure you do" (seething sarcasm), "I don't trust you" (smoldering suspicion),

"I know you are being treated wrong" (detrimental denial),
"I can't handle you" (emotional overheating), "It's all your
fault" (blame blasting), "You should/must/ought" ("should"
slamming), or "You will end up failing later on" (dooming
conclusions).

2. *Give yourself a reminder.* Some people find it helpful to tape
   a note on the car dashboard (just don't look at it while you
   are driving), the bathroom mirror, or their computer, reading "Stay aware" or "Pay attention" or "Remember to listen."
   One of my clients wore a blue elastic-band ribbon around
   her wrist to remind her to listen. She would look at it and
   think, "Why am I wearing this?" and then quickly remember and listen to herself.

3. *Write it down.* Just as Elena found out, there is a lot to be
   said for writing things down. So keep a small notebook in
   your purse, briefcase, or pocket. Putting your toxic thoughts
   in black and white really helps you capture what you are
   thinking. You may well be surprised at the sheer volume of
   toxic thoughts.

4. *Keep your feelings out of the way.* As you get in touch with
   your toxic thoughts, I realize that it is easy to let your feelings
   creep in, or even flood in. This is normal. I am asking you to
   take on the mind-set of detective or investigator—simply
   gather the information. It is crucial when identifying toxic
   thinking not to launch off into toxic feelings, or you will lose
   track of your thoughts. If you commit to understanding yourself and your child rather than punishing her, you will stay
   more objective. The goal here is to become more aware.

Step 2: Pay Attention to How You Feel Physically

I have been focusing so far on tuning in to your mind. Another way
to become more mindful is to tune in to your body. The link between our minds and bodies is well recognized. Studies of aging

show that reducing angst and worry improves health and increases longevity.

Many people are initially surprised to discover that their thoughts trigger physical reactions, even though the mind-body connection is expressed in our everyday language. We talk about "gut feelings" and how some people can even be a "pain in the butt."

When you pay attention to your body, you may notice that your back is killing you or your heart beats more strongly as soon as your kids are fighting. Or your daughter walks in and starts to clang cabinet doors and you instantly get a burning sensation in your stomach. See these as prime opportunities to connect what you're feeling in your body to what's going on in your mind. Watching your physical reactions, such as tightness in your chest or your head starting to pound, will show you your toxic thoughts as they occur, and the faster you will be able to calm yourself down.

The negative effects of toxic thoughts aren't all immediate, however. Whereas flaring toxic thoughts may trigger instantaneous physical reactions, slower-burning toxic thoughts can manifest themselves physically as well. Both types of toxic thoughts can leave you feeling exhausted and physically drained. Toxic thoughts don't simply go away without taking a toll on you. They stick, and they often make you sick.

Beth told me that every night her whole body would tense up at the sound of her ADHD son's impatient "mom, MOM, MOM!" "I would literally feel my jaw tightening up when Curt would provoke Sienna [his sister] and then carry on that he was the one always getting in trouble. I used to get pounding headaches as a result." A year of counseling helped Curt be less provocative. Yet it still took Beth some time to have fewer headaches. "It was like I had trained myself to tense up in preparation for his behavior, but then never untrained myself when he finally stopped being so disruptive."

Beth's experience is consistent with the work of the famous Russian scientist Ivan Pavlov, who would ring a bell every time he pre-

sented a dog with a steak. After doing this repeatedly, Pavlov found
the dog salivated upon just hearing the bell. We similarly develop
strong associations and expectations about our children. It's amazing how our bodies can be surprisingly reliable—and predictable!—
barometers of our thoughts and feelings. Table 5.1 provides the
physical cues that may be indicative of your toxic thoughts.

Table 5.1   Physical cues for toxic thoughts

sweaty palms	lethargy	ringing in ears
tense jaw	shaking of limbs	nausea
headache	quavering voice	insomnia
stomachache	blurred vision	neck or back ache
shortness of breath	loud voice	fatigue
grinding teeth	clenching fists	dizziness

Here are three important considerations to keep in mind as you
tune in to your body for clues to your toxic thinking:

1. *Know what being tense and being relaxed feel like.* In
   Chapter 4, I gave you a number of exercises to use to relax
   yourself. Not only is relaxation important, but it is also necessary to remind yourself what it feels like. As you quiet
   your mind, you will be more in tune with where the tension
   lies in your body. This will help you be more mindful in the
   moment of stressing out.
2. *Many of us are so tense, so much of the time, that we
   convince ourselves that it's normal and healthy.* Even
   feeling chronically on edge can begin to seem acceptable. It
   can be hard to tell when you're tensing up if you spend
   quite a bit of your day stressed out. Remind yourself, ran-
   domly, that you don't have to be so anxious. I personally
   have found this very helpful. I love it when I catch myself

and say, "Jeff, just chill out." Also, after work or before you go to bed, take a few moments and relax. Either sitting up or lying down, acknowledge each part of your body and relax it.

3. **When you note that your body is tense, try to find the source of your angst.** The two considerations above are for global mind-body awareness. To take it further, ask yourself, "Why am I holding my breath? Why are my shoulders so sore? What am I thinking about?" Stay mindful so that you choose your thoughts and to a large extent, your physical level of stress. Allow your focus on your body to show you what is happening with your thoughts.

A client of mine who jokingly referred to herself as "Stressed-Out Sheryl" became very good at learning how to "chill out." When she first came to see me, Sheryl had a laundry list of stressors and related physical complaints. These included headaches, stomach problems, occasional anxiety attacks, and muscle stiffness. Sheryl described herself as "falling apart at the seams."

Sheryl began to practice a wide range of relaxation exercises and strategies. One day, Sheryl shared how she used one of her new skills: "I simply go through my whole body and say, 'Now my knees are relaxed. And there are my arms. When my whole body is relaxed, I try to take note of how it feels to not be tense. I stay that way for a few minutes. Then, I tense my whole body and hold it for a few seconds. Then I release it." Eventually, she realized that she no longer was plagued by stress.

Step 3: Determine Your Triggers for Toxic Thinking

As parents, we all have hot buttons. These are the specific situations in which we are particularly prone to jumping to toxic thoughts. Common stressors are sassy back talk, messy rooms, entitlement, and motivational breakdowns. It's important to recognize what these triggers are so you'll be aware when you're most at risk for toxic thinking.

For Dorothy and Roberto, a trigger for both of them was comparing their son, Duane, to his cousins. Dorothy and Roberto felt Duane was lazy. They compared him to his hardworking but not as academically gifted cousins, and felt Duane should measure up better. Not surprisingly, Duane resented his parents' overzealous desire for him to "be like them."

Dorothy: *"After Duane was born we tried to do everything the right way to give this kid every advantage possible. Piano lessons, tutoring to help him with weak subjects—you name it and we did it. Things should have gotten better, but they didn't. I guess seeing Duane shut down and refuse to do his homework and be content with barely getting by in school means that he is a losing battle and that we are failures as parents."*

Roberto: *"I would think, 'I bust my ass for this kid. I grew up in the ghetto and had to scrape for everything, and my son just expects it all. It's bad enough that he doesn't even look at me when I talk to him. He should give me respect. Every time we tried to talk about it, it deteriorated into a screaming match, and he'd say things like, 'You always treat me like crap' and 'You don't care about my opinion . . . ' I think we were both scared when I suggested seeing a counselor because we knew we really needed it. But just last week he threw his phone at me when I tried to talk to him about his grades. He is putting a terrible strain on our marriage. Duane looks at me as being only a money machine. I feel like he doesn't respect me or care about my opinions. It has been a tough time for us."*

Duane definitely had fallen into some unhealthy avoidance strategies and was not working up to his potential at school. He also was hitting some all-time lows on the respect meter when interacting with his well-meaning parents. But, fortunately, Dorothy and Roberto were also able to recognize that Duane's struggles with school triggered toxic thinking on their part. Once they both were able to recognize that their thoughts on this issue had become toxic, they could step back and rethink their well-meaning but un-realistic expectations. Roberto went from "He doesn't even care about his future" to "Well, maybe Duane will consider community college. Even if he doesn't, being on his case is not going to help him." Interestingly, the more that Roberto and Dorothy worked on their own toxic thoughts, the more invested Duane eventually became in school. He ended up going to a year of community college and then successfully transferred to a four-year college where he earned an engineering degree.

Here are a few guidelines to help you identify your toxic-thought triggers:

1. ***Suspend yourself from the ceiling.*** Okay, hold on. Don't go running for a ladder and superglue. I am simply encouraging you to mentally watch your interactions with your child as they occur. Many of the parents I work with have found this visual really helpful. If you imagine yourself looking down at your child as you are interacting, then it will give you a more open and balanced perspective. Too often we fall into a role, such as taskmaster or homework enforcer, and the consequent power struggle is predictable. So watch the whole experience without getting sucked into it.

2. ***Keep track of your power struggles and conflicts.*** In Step 1 above, "Listen to Your Toxic Thoughts," I suggested keeping a notebook so you can write down your thoughts. This is a great way to see if there are one or two particular areas that are triggers for you. Do you and your child have a particular hot-button issue, such as homework, getting along with a sibling, or completion of household chores? If you find yourself having an argument around a recurring battle area, pay particular attention, as you will probably be having toxic thoughts. Many parents are surprised to discover how many toxic thoughts end up clustering around one area.

3. *Realize that your stressors will change*. Right now, your son claims he hates your husband, who is his stepfather. Your own thoughts about this give you big-time PFS. This may come from thinking toxically ("He does not appreciate anything. He should be thankful that I married such a good guy."). In the next year or so, with acceptance and the passage of time, tensions could lessen between your son and your new husband. At that point, you may find yourself reacting to your son's new group of friends whom you think are not the best influence. My point is that parental concerns and parenting relationships go in and out of stressful periods. Know that staying on top of one stressor doesn't guarantee there won't be others that need your attention.

Many times, what sets off toxic thinking is one of our personal issues, or "baggage." Most of us don't like to deal with our past "stuff." Why? Because no one likes to revive past hurts or recognize mistakes. But I do try to acknowledge my baggage because I know it's better for me if I do. I know that when I don't have a sense of how that "stuff" predisposes me to certain toxic thoughts, it is like walking in the dark—you keep bumping into things without any warning. As I said earlier, "What you resist will persist."

For better or worse, we are heavily influenced by our families in terms of how we approach parenting. Most of us are oblivious to this. For example, the way your family expressed affection will shape your expectations and perceptions in ways that are probably not obvious to you. If you grew up with a parent who was very critical, you may judge your own children, and be prone to "always or never" thoughts or "'should' slamming." This could lead your child to be evasive and defensive with you.

I am pleased to tell you that you can sort out issues that are impairing your thinking now. All it takes is a willingness to become mindful of your baggage. One of the easiest ways is to recognize the patterns. If your kids continually react to you in the same ways and you hear the same negative feedback ("You're always yelling" or "You don't listen to me"), maybe it is time to look in the mirror. This isn't about being self-critical or blaming your parents for your own parenting hassles. It's about understanding yourself on a deeper level so you can improve your relationships.

Step 4: Remain Calm

A big reason to avoid toxic thinking is that it triggers toxic feelings, like anger, frustration, and resentment. Remaining calm is not only important for identifying and controlling toxic thoughts but also imperative for controlling feelings.

Parental anger is a major problem. Child abuse, rooted in anger, is a significant issue in our society. I am grateful that my toxic thoughts and feelings did not lead me to physically abuse my children. But they made me into a serious hard-ass. And it was not healthy. I was verbally aggressive and used harsh restraining tactics. It took extended effort to reconnect with my kids after I detoxified.

Before we go further, check out "You Control Your Feelings" to understand just how powerful feelings are in our lives.

You Control Your Feelings

Feelings are very intense and powerful. Our feelings are manipulated by the media, politicians, our children, our parents, our co-workers, even our pets (remember how you felt when you walked in and saw your dog's "accident" on the new rug?). Sometimes it is tempting to believe that we are simply passive beings whose fate is at the mercy of those who can influence our feelings.

But I don't think this is really the case. Think about it: Have you ever appropriately hit the brakes when you realized that the other driver was not going to let you pull out? Have you

ever talked yourself out of buying something you could not afford even though you really wanted it? Have you ever
wanted to scream at or punch someone in public but held
your tongue and your fist? In all these cases, your self-control
kept you from acting on your feelings. You had discipline and
strength. You can do that as a parent, too, with self-
awareness and self-control. That's being a grown-up.

Sadly, too many of us do not apply such discipline when
we interact with our children. Our hot buttons and triggers set
us off. But they don't have to. *Always remember that by controlling our toxic thinking, we can control our feelings.*

• •

Your Head Counts Just as Much as Your Heart

When your child's behavior annoys you and you go toxic, it is important to remember that it's not the situation but rather your *interpretation* of the situation that makes the difference between
harmony and chaos. You can choose to interpret the words or behaviors of your child toxically (unrealistically) or nontoxically
(realistically).

As I mentioned in Chapter 3, the idea that we can change and
shape our own thinking has been rigorously studied in the field of
cognitive therapy. Cognitive therapists show clients how they can
systematically train themselves to think their way out of the shackles of depression, anxiety, anger, and other problematic emotions.
The key here is to be aware that thoughts cause feelings and that
by changing your underlying thinking you can change how you feel.
This can revolutionize parenting for you. This new ability to think
more clearly, with more balance, and increasingly positively will
also improve your relationship with yourself, your significant other,
friends and colleagues, and everyone else in your life.

Mindful parenting takes discipline and maturity. Being self-disciplined as a parent means facing and working through those troubling thoughts and feelings that you struggle with. ***The more self-disciplined you are, the less you will have to discipline your child****. Why? Because you will have fewer toxic thoughts for your child to react against in the first place.

Yes, I know your kids will test you, and often conflict will seem to arise out of the blue. After all, that's part of a kid's job—to see what he can get away with. But the way you choose to interpret and react to your child's instigations, provocations, manipulations, machinations, undulations, and all other "-ations" will set the tone, whether it will be calm problem solving or a chaotic emotional disaster.

I have worked closely with well over two thousand parents and children and have seen so many parents break free from the shackles of toxic thinking. Their kids have become more manageable, and these families experienced much more joy.

But don't think I mean for you to put on rose colored glasses and ignore the things your child does that bug you. No way! Ignoring frustrations keeps you on the PFS plan—where you bottle it up and explode later. And the results will leave both you and your kids feeling awful (and you awfully guilty).

Two Wolves

One evening an old Cherokee told his grandson about a battle that goes on inside people. He said, "My son, the battle is between two 'wolves' inside us all. One is Evil. It is anger, envy, jealousy, sorrow, regret, greed, arrogance, self-pity, guilt, resentment, inferiority, lies, false pride, superiority, and ego. The other is Good. It is joy, peace, love, hope, serenity, humility, kindness, benevolence, empathy, generosity, truth, compassion and faith."

The grandson thought about it for a minute and then asked his grandfather: "Which wolf wins?"

The old Cherokee simply replied, "The one you feed."

This was one of those "mass e-mails" forwarded to me by a client. I love this story because it emphasizes the power of how we choose to look at things.

As you learn about toxic thoughts, realize that you, like the Cherokee in this tale, have the choice to feed them or replace them with more healthy thinking patterns.

● ●

Alternative Thoughts Lead to Alternative Outcomes

Rather than ignoring your toxic thoughts, dispute them and develop alternative ways of thinking. I can't stress enough that if you make the change to a healthier, nontoxic way of thinking, in most cases your child will respond positively. As you will soon see, alternative thoughts will lead to alternative feelings and new and better interactions.

Randy was a successful computer consultant and father of two demanding children with ADHD and learning disabilities. When he and his wife first consulted me, Randy made it clear that he was a "logic man." Randy had seen a couples' counselor with his first wife some years ago. He felt the experience was not helpful; he found it too nondirective and "all over the place."

Randy also made it clear to me that he was along only to support Lynette, his current wife. He wanted her to "get some tools that work to manage the kids." Randy looked me right in the eye and said, "No offense, Dr. Jeff, but I don't think I really believe in your approach. I am just giving my wife the benefit of the doubt." He added, "Parents these days coddle their kids *wayyyyy* too much, and the place to be looking is [at] what your kids do, and not what you think as a parent."

As Randy continued speaking, he became quite animated. He asserted to me that neither he nor his family *needed* to be in my office for counseling. I then surprised Randy because I agreed with him that he and his family did not need counseling. I said that counseling may be beneficial but that it certainly was not needed. Randy then told me he liked the way I responded, honestly and nondefensively.

I then asked Randy an important question: "If I would have responded to you in a defensive way, based on toxic thoughts, then would that have influenced how you feel about me right now?" Randy replied, "Absolutely. Of course it would." I just smiled. From that moment, Randy was very open to looking at his own thinking patterns, as he realized their impact.

Once parents learn about toxic thoughts, many say to me that they now wish they had a fresh start to do parenting all over again. To that I can only say, "Hey, much better late than never." I have heard many stories of long-standing negative feelings between parents and children, sometimes even lasting lifetimes.

You now have the opportunity to express your thoughts and emotions, as a parent, in a more centered, healthy way. You will be able to parent your child in a less reactive, and calmer, fashion. Let's now arm you with alternatives to make this happen. Here are some tools to help you do just that.

Prove It Yourself

The way to develop healthy alternatives to your toxic thoughts is simple: **You need to gather evidence to dispute them.** Remember, toxic thoughts are simply distorted explanations for your child's actions, words, and behaviors. What most parents don't ever realize is that challenging their toxic thoughts with sound, positive, alternative explanations based on evidence and not emotion will make their relationship with their child stronger and more rewarding.

When it comes to toxic thoughts like "He's constantly challenging me" or "She is always disrespectful," I say put your money
where your mouth is but with a twist. Prove to yourself that your
child is *not* always being disrespectful, disobedient, dishonest, or
any of that "dis-" stuff.

Wait a minute! Shouldn't that be the other way around? Don't
you need to prove that your son is constantly challenging you so you
don't let him "get away" with problem behaviors? No, and here's the
reason: Once you're in the throes of toxic thinking, you're already
focused on evidence that supports your belief that he's constantly
challenging (like when he told you last week that you are never
fair and the week before when he said you're always mean . . .).
Instead, you need to gather evidence *against* your toxic thoughts by
challenging your interpretation of your child's words or actions (as
when just yesterday, out of the blue, he agreed with your decision
to let his brother watch a television show). As you take this critical step in developing toxic-thought-busting alternatives, keep the
following in mind:

- *Find at least three exceptions to the behavior.* Toxic
  thoughts tend to be all encompassing. So whatever types of
  toxic thoughts you are having, find exceptions to the rule. It is
  unlikely your child is always challenging or completely defiant.

  Lance thought that Martin, his fourteen-year-old son, was
  "unappreciative of everything, and always wanting more."
  However, when I encouraged Lance to think of positive exceptions, it, surprisingly, wasn't all that difficult: "Martin was
  very strong after his mother's cancer surgery. He's also been
  good to his younger brother."

  As Lance focused on the alternatives and embraced Martin's strengths, an interesting shift occurred. Martin literally
  started to act more appreciative. Lance then had even more
  evidence to challenge his perceptions of Martin's ingratitude.

That's the magic of challenging toxic thoughts. The more you challenge them, the easier it becomes.

Like Lance, you too will feel empowered when you look for the positive exceptions to the toxic rule. One or two examples may convince you, but finding three or even more is best.

- **Pretend you're not his or her parent.** Whoa, hold on and reread this one more closely. Many parents sit in my office and share that other parents, teachers, music teachers, Boy Scout leaders, and karate instructors think their child is wonderful. They don't see the challenging side of kids who are not their own.

  Bearing this in mind, imagine that you are not your child's parent. I know—this may be a nice fantasy on some days. But on a more serious note, what I am asking you to do is to take your emotions out of the picture, or at least put them on the shelf. So imagine yourself as a neighbor or friend who has struggles with her own kids, too. Realize that all parents have trying times with their kids. Now pretend that you are another parent singing praises about your child. This will open you up to other positive perspectives on your child.

  I have a close friend who had some major problems with one of his daughters, now an adult. This friend of mine is one of the most easygoing, cheerful people I know. Yet he nearly swerved off the road while driving one day when we began discussing his girl. Fortunately, we did not crash, even though he had quickly switched into toxic-thinking mode. As I calmly and sincerely shared the positive attributes and qualities of his daughter, he calmed down. My friend had a flood of long-buried positive feelings toward her and took her out to dinner that evening. He began to listen and focus on her wonderful qualities. After that experience, his trips to the land of toxic thinking were far fewer and much shorter in duration. Suffice it to say, this father and daughter also became much closer than they had ever been.

By looking at your child through someone else's eyes, you will see the hidden merits in her character as well. The more you detoxify, the more empathy you will have to understand your child's point of view or position. A deeper understanding of your child's perspective will often help remove the roadblocks as well as the underlying toxic thoughts. Empathy— especially deep empathy—is the emotional glue that holds parents and children together. Understanding your child is as important as loving him. Remember, understanding is often the missing link for liking your child. To really help you get into this mind-set, imagine that you are being given fifty thousand dollars to find the evidence to defend your child against your own toxic thoughts (now that's a real fruitful labor of love!).

- ***Remember the big picture.*** Many televisions have the capacity to show a small picture within a big picture. A colleague of mine once told me to visualize negative concerns as a small picture and put a big picture of more positive thoughts around it. If you keep the big picture in mind about your child, you will have big-time success challenging your toxic thoughts. Make your toxic thoughts the small picture and expand your alternative positive thoughts to fit the big screen. This visual will help you keep your thoughts in a more helpful, healthy, and positive perspective. The beauty of this exercise is that it illustrates that you don't have to feel pressure to make your toxic thoughts completely vanish. Simply focus on shrinking them down in size and expanding the positive alternative thoughts. This alone will leave you feeling more in control of your feelings.

- **Write it down**. It will help you to see your evidence in black and white. Think about how good it feels when you've had positive things written about you. Seeing a strong work review certainly feels good, doesn't it? How about the teachers who gave you good grades? Writing down positive statements about your child expands your mind for mindful parenting. Try it first on yourself—I'm giving you permission to toot your own horn. Write down some specific positive things about yourself in the space below:

_____

_____

_____

_____

_____

_____

Please give yourself this gift. It could be anything that matters to you, like the time you volunteered at your daughter's school or the appreciation you get from other parents for coaching your son's soccer team. Or your list may include how you're seen as a team player and a problem solver at work. If doing this helps you feel good about yourself, why not give this gift to your child?

Eyeing the Prize

As you become more mindful of toxic thinking, an amazing transformation will occur. You will realize that you *do* have a choice about your feelings when it comes to your child—a choice not to feel the anger, rejection, or frustration that toxic thinking inevitably leads to. Sure, giving in to your toxic thoughts in the short term is a lot easier, and it can even feel good. But you and your child have to live with the long-term emotionally unhealthy consequences. And then you're stuck with persistent PFS.

I like to think of parenting mindfulness as the opposite of toxic thinking. Toxic thinking is automatic, habitlike, one-sided, rigid, and destructive to parenting relationships. Parenting mindfulness, on the other hand, is flowing and flexible; it promotes acceptance and empathy, helping your child's all-important self-esteem grow strong.

But This Is Not Easy for Me

Maybe you are feeling a few toxic thoughts toward me. I hope not. Perhaps, however, you fear you won't be able to get ahold of those toxic thoughts when your child is being difficult with you.

Madeline, the exasperated mother of defiant fourteen-year-old Joy, leaned forward on my couch during a session. Her husband, Claude, looked at her and encouraged her to calm down. Madeline said, "Dr. Jeff, I was brought up by a German father and an Irish mother. They just told us what to do, and we knew better than to question them." She went on and said, "I want to give Joy the best and stay calm, but it is hard to do. My real desire is to take everything I can away from her as consequences and teach her a lesson or two."

Previously, Joy had been sent to live with Madeline's father, a retired assistant public school principal. Whereas the plan was for Grandpa to get Joy to behave, all that resulted was Grandpa and Grandma were worn out and at their wit's end. Joy was bounced back home. Fortunately, tensions eased once Madeline let go of her toxic thoughts and discovered that she did not need to be a consequence-hungry parent anymore. (I will discuss consequences further in Chapter 8.)

It may not be easy, but in order to remain mindful, you've got to keep yourself from getting angry or frustrated. You've got to keep your cool. Here are three more suggestions for remaining calm and not allowing yourself to be swept away by toxic thoughts:

1. ***Give yourself a pep talk.*** Remind yourself that if you can talk yourself into parenting angst, then you can talk yourself out of it. Say to yourself, "I'm feeling mad/sad/rejected/hurt because of a toxic thought that may not reflect reality." Then ask yourself, "Do I want to have control over my thoughts or do I want them to control me?" Who would choose the latter? Also ask yourself, "If I keep going off on my kids, then how will I feel years down the road?"

2. ***Pick an alternative ending.*** One day one of my kids was giving me a hard time, and I started to lose my cool—until I had this incredible revelation: I did not have to. This was a magical moment for me. As they say in Alcoholics Anonymous, "Nothing changes if nothing changes." So I picked a calm, firm, noncontrolling approach. And surprise, surprise, I got a new, positive outcome.

3. ***Use a mantra.*** Keeping yourself from feeling a toxic feeling *can* be as simple as recognizing that you're having a toxic thought and repeating a simple phrase, or mantra, like, *Okay, slow down.* Trust me, repeating short phrases over and over again works to help you create a new thinking habit. Remember, you thought your way into frustration with your child, so you have to practice thinking your way out of it. A little phrase like "Okay, this is not at all horrible," "Calm down, this may not be what it seems," or "Wait a minute—is this toxic thinking?" can act as a gentle reminder to remain mindful and not to dive into the tank of toxic thinking.

To Sum It All Up

In the next two chapters I am going to take you into the
trenches in the war on your toxic thoughts. Now that you
have learned to become a more mindful parent, you will be
able to apply the forthcoming tools effectively. As you read,
keep the following points in mind:

- Being a mindful parent will help you work smarter rather
  than harder because you will learn how to identify and
  take responsibility for your own counterproductive thoughts
  and feelings.
- Your physical reactions are important signals that reveal what
  is going on in your mind.
- Staying calm and being vigilant for toxic thoughts will help
  you stay in charge of your feelings.
- Once you create the habit of listening to toxic thoughts,
  you will be amazed at how little you were aware of what
  you've been telling yourself about your child.

Chapter 6

Douse "Slow-Burning" Toxic Thoughts

HERE'S A BIG QUESTION: Now that you are more mindful of your toxic thoughts, what are you going to do about them? I hope you will zap them right out of your head.

In this and the following chapter, I am going to show you how to dispute and remove those troubling toxic thoughts. As you remove the garbage from your mind, you will be able to replace it with balanced, healthy thoughts. Those helpful thoughts are what I refer to as "alternatives." By alternatives I mean new, fairer, and more flexible ways to look at your child's words, attitudes, and actions.

When you are frustrated, it becomes hard for you to understand why your child is being so challenging. Toxic thoughts wreak havoc on your ability to calm down and solve problems. The five toxic thoughts addressed in this chapter I call "slow burning," because they tend to fester and build up over time. Parents with these thoughts may act distant, feel resentful, and be less emotionally connected with their children.

In Chapter 7, I will address the flaring toxic thoughts. They are more incendiary, and tend to lead to verbal outbursts. Please keep in mind that any toxic thoughts have the potential to either fester or flare up. The general dichotomy presented in these two chapters is more conceptual than absolute.

The key strategy to defeat either slower-burning or flaring toxic thoughts is the use of alternatives. The relaxation strategies discussed in Chapter 4 and mindfulness strategies presented in Chapter 5 are both crucial to apply as you use alternatives. The relaxation strategies are especially vital to counter flaring toxic thoughts.

The sad reality is that being a toxic thinker sucks up a lot of time and energy—more than you ever realized! I know it is tempting to point your finger (literally and figuratively) at your child and blame her when you're upset. You may be asking, "Why do I have to look at what I am thinking and doing if she is being bratty in the first place?" I just ask you to remember that when you point your finger at your child, you are also pointing your finger away from your own heart. This works against you because the best parenting you can offer comes straight from your heart.

It is not until you get control of what goes on in your head that you will gain control of your child when she is out of control. Yes, being a more rational and centered parent takes some discipline and work. If your child is giving you a hard time, you certainly have the right to feel burned out. But even if it feels good to go toxic and blow off steam in the short term, you are only creating more angst and tension in the long run. Let's now discuss the five slow-burning toxic-thought patterns so you can see exactly how to create alternative thoughts for each of them.

1. Unleashing Yourself from the "Always or Never" Trap

In Chapter 3, Julie's negative, all-encompassing thoughts about and frustrations with Rachel, her thirteen-year-old daughter, left her painfully ensnared in the "always or never" trap. At the heart of her toxic frustrations were the thoughts that Rachel "is never satisfied with anything I do for her," "is always creating drama," and "does not care about anyone but herself."

Julie had realized in her sessions with me that her "always or never" thoughts led her to see her daughter unfairly. Stressed out with her all-or-nothing thinking, Julie was quite game to learn how to dispute these toxic thoughts. Julie was initially in tears, as she acknowledged, "Dr. Jeff, this is cruel for me to say, but I just can't stand Rachel on some days. She antagonizes me to no end and seems to enjoy doing it." Julie had most recently felt frustration when Rachel bitterly complained that the new pair of jeans that Julie had bought her were "pathetic and ugly."

With my encouragement, Julie began shifting mental gears and took on the job of defending her daughter against her own belief that Rachel was constantly unappreciative. We explored the various situations where this was not the case:

- Rachel told her mom that she appreciated her help in preparing for a history test.
- The previous week, Rachel told Julie that she liked the dress Julie had purchased for her younger sister (showing a capacity to appreciate positive gestures for others in her family).
- Rachel recently ceased complaining about how her friends were all "users and losers" when Julie reassured her that the junior high school years are not easy.
- Rachel agreed when her mom told her that she had a hard time expressing what she liked.
- As Julie calmed down, she reminded herself that Rachel had a negative body image and felt very self-conscious about her clothing.

As Julie focused on her daughter Rachel's grateful and positive behaviors, she made a powerful discovery: even more evidence of Rachel's appreciation! For example, Julie remembered how proudly Rachel referred to her as "my mom" in public. This may seem small to anyone else, but as Julie smiled and reflected on it, she felt fulfilled. Even more thoughts of Rachel's consideration of others and good qualities began to emerge. At first they trickled, but soon they poured into Julie's mind. Clearly, it wasn't so hard to come up with at least six pieces of evidence to use against her toxic thoughts. Just to drive home more alternatives, I had Julie write them down:

1. Rachel is expressive about how she likes it when I make lasagna.
2. She thanked me two weeks ago for taking her and her friend to the mall.
3. Rachel apologized to me the other day for when she was irritable.
4. She responsibly watches her younger sister when I do my kickboxing workout.
5. Rachel was incredibly patient and supportive when my father died last year.
6. She wrote a recent English paper saying what a wonderful mother I am.

There, in black and white, was the evidence Julie needed to seal the deal, and to stop her toxic thinking. Julie stepped back from her distorted thoughts and saw the reality: Rachel may not be an easy daughter, but she is not ALWAYS unappreciative. In fact, Rachel has the capacity to be caring, loving, and grateful. And here's the best part: Julie almost instantly lost her anger. "After looking at all this evidence, how could I be mad at her?" Julie asked me. "In fact, I appreciate her even more. I feel like I should apologize for even having that toxic thought in the first place." Julie then paused and added, "Oops, I just did the 'should' thing. I guess being hard on myself is not helpful."

Julie also found an unexpected bonus: She began to notice less friction and more harmony in her marriage. Donald, her husband, had been resentful, in the past, of being "stuck in the middle" of the conflicts between his wife and daughter. As Julie detoxified her thoughts, Donald admitted and dropped his own secret judgment: "Julie never gives this kid a break." As happens so often, when toxic thinking goes out the window in one relationship, it disappears elsewhere too.

This kind of profound transformation is not unusual. You're probably tired of hearing this, but I'll say it again because it's so important: The key here is to be aware that thoughts cause feelings and that by changing the underlying thinking you can actually change how you feel. By challenging and overcoming your toxic thinking, you will rediscover the positive qualities in your child. You will not only feel more joy in being a parent but also feel better about yourself. Most important, your child will sense this change in you.

Looking at the evidence and feeling more positively toward her daughter helped Julie focus on the big picture—all of Rachel's expressions of appreciation over a long period of time—and not simply on a few unappreciative moments. Julie's other toxic thoughts, that Rachel was always creating drama and that all she cared about was herself, also disappeared. Often, once parents dislodge and discard one toxic thought, the others automatically disappear as well. Not surprisingly, Rachel's dramatic antics and self-absorbed tendencies also lessened as she felt a renewed sense of understanding from and positive connection to her mother.

When we feel threatened, we can lose sight of the big picture— that our children are well intended, and they desperately need us to believe in them; and underneath their inappropriate behaviors are often confusion, emotional pain, and fear. Please keep these "big-picture" truths in mind:

- No parent or child is perfect.
- Problems don't usually last forever.
- Parental understanding is the best strategy for regaining control when children are out of line.

Table 6.1   Going from always or never
to reasonable and realistic

Always or Never Toxic Words	Reasonable and Realistic Words
Always	Sometimes, at times, tends to, more than I would like
Never	Occasionally, not as much as I would like
All the time	In some cases, many times
Nothing	Not as much as I would like, right now, some things
Everything	This one thing or these couple of things

Armed with the evidence that Rachel "does, at times, appreci-ate what I do for her," Julie is now able to put a more realistic spin on her thoughts. She is now able to calmly look at the evidence and put Rachel's actions into their proper perspective. Now when Rachel whines, Julie tells herself, "Rachel is struggling with being a teenager, but that does not mean she is out to make me miser-able. She really had some good days this past week." Sometimes Julie slips into the "always or never" trap again, but when she does, she now has the alternatives to zap those thoughts.

More Alternatives to the "Always or Never" Trap

Consider table 6.1. Some words and phrases are obvious red flags for "always or never" thoughts. If you replace these toxic words with more reasonable and realistic ones, your all-or-nothing think-ing will all but disappear.

In fact, parents I work with tell me they are amazed at the dra-matic, positive difference that a few words can make. They quickly realize that once they break the habit of using rigid words, toxic thinking is practically eliminated. Table 6.2 shows concrete exam-ples of alternatives to the "always or never" trap.

Table 6.2   Using evidence to build alternative
thoughts to the always or never trap

Toxic Thoughts	Evidence to the Contrary	Alternative Thoughts
"He *never* listens to me."	"That's not true. Just the other day, he agreed to put away his toys when I asked him to."	"Just because he does not listen as much as I'd like does not mean there is anything wrong with him. He is a great kid and has shown his ability to cope by being so kind to his little sister."
"He is *always* moody."	"Last week, he made me and my friends laugh when he kept saying that tongue twister over and over."	"He is moody at times, and that can be a signal for me to remember how he gets frustrated with school. I can call him on his moodiness without getting sucked into it."
"*Nothing* he says is true."	"He often does tell me the truth. And I have yelled at him too much after he has been honest with me."	"He lies because he is afraid to be honest with me. I will work on letting him know if I question whether he is telling the truth, but I will use a less aggressive approach."

But Hold on, My Child Really Does Always Act So Difficult

You might be tempted to think that your situation is the exception. Naturally, many of my clients challenge me and say, "But he *really* always does this" or "She *really* never does that."

My response is to take these parents back in time to when their child was first born. I ask if the upsetting behavior occurred then too. More often than not, it did not. Most parents remember that precious little bundle of joy with a warm smile. So now they have concrete evidence for the case that "always" is not true. Even in the rare cases in which there were problems from day one, like having a colicky newborn, it certainly does not mean there were not also positive experiences.

The bottom line is, challenging toxic thoughts changes your perspective—for the better. When you develop alternative explanations and gather evidence, you are naturally encouraged to see your child's good qualities and not just the negative ones. When you are able to step back and be more realistic, you are often able to be more accepting of your child's annoying habits. You may decide "It's not the biggest deal in the world" and let it go.

But It Really Bugs Me . . .

You may also decide to further pursue the issue that's bothering you with your child. Maybe it would be helpful to have a school psychologist evaluate your child for that persistent academic avoidance. Yet even if you get your child evaluated, getting schoolwork done may continue to be a challenge. In my previous book *10 Days to a Less Distracted Child*, I provided a powerful ten-day program for parents to help children of all ages effectively overcome distractibility problems. I also provide references of other books and resources at the end of this book. Rest assured that if your child's academic issues or other concerns continue to bug you, then you are only human.

The point is that detoxifying your thinking does not mean that nothing about your kids will ever bother you again. That's not realistic. Rather, disputing your toxic thoughts with alternatives allows you to connect with the real issues, and react in a way that is more supportive and fair. The combination of relaxation, mindfulness, and alternatives works together and takes you, and your relationship with your child, to more joyful places. You will see your child with more clarity and see issues in a less skewed way, and problems will feel more manageable.

In your more mindful state you can catch and stop yourself from expressing, and most important dwelling on, your toxic thoughts and instead express yourself in a more productive manner. As Julie told me, "Yes, I do feel that Rachel still can be melodramatic and can be self-centered, but now I don't phrase it, 'You're always melodramatic or selfish.' Instead I say, 'I would really appreciate it if you could speak to me in a kinder way like I know you are capable of.' And it usually works. Even if she does not respond immediately and just rolls her eyes, I am letting her know my concern without letting my toxic thoughts deliver my words with a sledgehammer. The less emotionally attached I am to getting a certain response from her, the smoother things go between us. More often than not, she will soften and we talk it out. Becoming mindful helped me realize that she's not blind to what I do for her; she's just being a teenager."

2. Letting Go of Label Gluing

In Chapter 3 I discussed Lazy Lenny and Careless and Irresponsible Jane. Although their labels were different, the impact on each of them was the same—they were inwardly outraged.

If you recall from Chapter 3, labels are an easy and convenient way for parents to process information and express it. If you think about it, parents are "on duty" twenty-four hours a day, seven days a week. So I do understand that you need all the time-saving ways that you can get. Yet toxic labels leave your child locked into a negative identity. And labeled kids are usually fraught with frustration, hurt, anger, and resentment. They will be demotivated from making positive changes. Many adults lament how they themselves were labeled as children. Toxic labels leave toxic baggage.

For example, Kevin was an adult I worked with who, as a child, was told by his sisters' friends that he was ugly. Although many women found him attractive, he wasn't so confident. When dating, if a normal disconnect arose, he convinced himself that it was because he was ugly. As Kevin worked with me in counseling, he stopped being so self-critical. He relabeled himself attractive and desirable. Soon after, he met his future wife.

If you glue a negative label on your child, she will live up to it. Alternatively, if you replace the negative label with a more positive one, she will live up to that too. It may be hard for you to lose the detrimental label in your mind completely. In that case I encourage you to add a much bigger one that is more positive and let it over-shadow the negative one, like Dena, who learned to see her daughter Shannon as curious rather than nosy.

As in the case of zapping any toxic thought, you must first gather evidence to dispute the label. You have to be honest with yourself and admit to what you're *really* saying. For example, thinking, calling, or both thinking *and* calling your child "lazy" or "careless" is hurtful. A child often hears this as "loser." If you doubt this, then try the golden rule on yourself in the following exercise:

Reexamining Your Own Past Label

Think of a negative label you were given during your child-hood. It could have been from a parent, teacher, relative, coach, or anyone else.

What was the label?

To what extent did it bother you to be labeled in this way?

How did you react to that label (for example, did you rebel, did you try to ignore it, did you try to live up to it out of spite)?

How did it impact your self-esteem?

How long did the emotional damage last from that negative label?

I challenged Lenny's dad to look at the big picture and gather evidence against his lazy label. He then realized that Lenny's black belt in karate and holding a part-time job suggested that Lenny did have motivation. It just was not as strong for school as it was in his extracurricular activities.

If you recall, Jane's parents, especially her dad, had regarded her as careless. Her parents had a major problem differentiating be-

Table 6.3

Label	What You're Really Saying
"You're lazy."	"I don't think you will be successful."
	"You can't ever get yourself motivated."
	"I don't approve of how you deal with the world."
"You're a pig."	"You're dirty."
	"You don't have any pride in yourself or your surroundings."
"You're selfish."	"All you care about is you."
	"You don't have the ability to see anyone else's needs at all."
"You're careless."	"You don't know how to do things well."
	"You never consider anything carefully."
"You're a crybaby."	"Your feelings are too strong and should not be acknowledged."
	"You can't handle anything challenging."
	"Your feelings don't really count."
"You're insensitive."	"You don't realize that other people have feelings."
	"You can't understand anything."

tween what Jane could and could not do. This is very common to parents of any child and especially those with attention deficit hyperactivity disorder and learning disabilities. Seeing how Jane took care of her child gave them a new appreciation of her.

Let's take a further look at some other labels and how they may be perceived by children in table 6.3.

I have often seen parents negatively label their children, even though they faced similar issues when they were younger. Jane's father, Ralph, also struggled with ADHD and as a result had become hypervigilant about organization. Ralph later admitted to me that he felt threatened by Jane's organizational chaos because it made

Table 6.4   More alternatives to toxic labels

Toxic Labels	Positive Reframing Labels
Impossible	Challenging
Immature	Still growing up
Brat	Difficult in this situation
Impatient	Easily frustrated by waiting
Temperamental	Struggling with appropriately expressing anger; intense
Shy	Cautious
Nosy	Curious
Liar	Scared to tell the truth
Calculating	Deliberate
Anal	Careful
Pushy	Enthusiastic
Nuts or Crazy	Unique
Stubborn	Determined
Selfish	Valuing himself
Jealous	Caring and protective
Unmotivated	Laid-back; motivationally blocked
Controlling	Confident
Passive	Accepting
Crazy	Frustrated and confused

him feel that he gave her bad genes. As Ralph saw from Jane's responsible handling of her pregnancy, she was far from careless.

I have shared with parents the negative labels presented in table 6.4, which I use to help them reframe their negative labels into more positive ones. I encourage you to be very careful about how you think about and express yourself to your child. Please note the exercise that follows the table.

Exercise: Replacing Negative Labels with Positive Ones

Remember that adage "Give a child a label and he will live up to it"? Now is your chance to break the labels that damage your child's self-esteem. Using table 6.4, try to identify any negative labels that you apply to your child. Now using the spaces below, place your negative labels on each top line, and then write a more positive label below, as well as any evidence you have to support it. Please see the sample ("temperamental") at the beginning to help get you started.

Negative label and underlying thinking:
Temperamental: She is so hard to talk to and gets moody so easily.

Positive-label alternative and underlying thinking:
Intense: Yes, she is not easy to talk to. Yet she can be very caring and sweet. Just because she gets riled does not mean it is fair to label her.

Negative label and underlying thinking:
_____
_____

Positive-label alternative and underlying thinking:
_____
_____

Negative label and underlying thinking:
_____
_____

Positive-label alternative and underlying thinking:
_____
_____

Negative label and underlying thinking:
_____
_____

Positive-label alternative and underlying thinking:
_____
_____

Keep in mind that toxic labels can be an offshoot of "always or never" thinking. This is because "always or never" thinking can convince parents that the child's identity is entirely negative.

. . . .

Negative Labels Are Not Healthy Motivators

There is a minority of parents who pride themselves on using negative labels to motivate their kids. I have met adults who remember, as children, being told that they were "a hopeless case" or "would never amount to anything." These adults may have vowed to become the opposite, yet often this comes with a tragic price: a shattered parent-child relationship. The old Johnny Cash song "A Boy Named Sue" tells the story of a boy whose father gave him a girl's name. The man wanted his son to become tough and self-reliant. Not surprisingly, the son had a rough life because of his first name. When the son grew up, he sought out his absent father and confronted him, and they fought. Although they made up and miraculously overcame years of hostility and rift, Sue vowed, "If I ever have a son, I'll name him Bill, George—anything but Sue!" Trust me, success spurred by love and support is less emotionally costly than success spurred by shame.

Remember that you can detoxify those labels. By finding positive evidence, you will be armed with alternatives to drive the negative labels out of your mind. And the more you find positive labels, the more you will find positive evidence to support them. Once you peel off that toxic label, the more you will catch your child's healthy, appropriate behaviors, and the more he will continue to act that way.

3. Silencing Your Seething Sarcasm

A thirteen-year-old client had parents who were sarcastic with him about his ineffectual efforts to play sports. I asked this boy what impact their comments had, and he said, "I get pissed off, and I just want to mess up in baseball."

By definition, sarcasm is caustic. Light sarcasm once in a while may not be hurtful. But a steady diet can be very demoralizing. I have been sarcastic with my own kids. The results were not pretty, and I am grateful I learned to put a lid on it.

Jordan was a fifteen-year-old boy with ADHD. His mother and father had fallen prey to sarcasm in response to his habitual defiance. Despite his difficulties in school, Jordan maintained that he would be a "big-ass boss dude" in years to come. One day his father snapped back, "Yeah, Jordan, like you will really end up being a boss someday. You can't even reliably take out the garbage. How are you going to take care of other people?"

In response, Jordan ran away and did not return until the following morning. That night he literally slept in the woods. That was fourteen years ago, and I am happy to report that at last update, Jordan had been promoted to being a boss at a large accounting firm.

In the time we worked together, Jordan's parents changed their thinking with powerful alternatives that got them out of the quicksands of sarcasm. These included:

- Even though Jordan dishes it out, that does not mean we have to snipe back.
- Our sarcastic urges are really just signals for us to be more patient and understanding.
- Jordan's problems are not going to look like this forever, and we need to make sure we don't mock him for struggling.
- Sarcasm feels good in the moment, but it creates a painful emotional rift.

Table 6.5 shows more examples of how to defeat seething sarcasm. These alternatives allow for empathy and support rather than letting you fall into cynicism and despair.

Table 6.5   More alternatives to seething sarcasm

Toxic Thoughts	Evidence to the Contrary	Alternative Thoughts
"Sure you studied, if you call talking on the phone a study of how to mess up your grades."	"He has always been a multitasking type of kid. Teasing him about how he studies just makes things worse."	"I have a right to be frustrated because he could work smarter, not just harder. He is more likely to hear me, however, if I stop with my seething sarcasm."
"You dress sleazy like that and then expect boys to respect you? Yeah, right."	"She is not the only one dressing like that."	"I know she is experimenting with the way she dresses. Like most teen girls, she has difficulties with competitive friends and her own body image."
"With that attitude nobody's going to put up with you. I feel sorry for the girl you marry."	"Deep down under his bravado he is scared. He admitted this to me a few weeks ago. It's just hard to remember how much he is hurting."	"He is actually fiercely loyal and protective of those he loves. It's best if I don't say anything else that could hurt him."

Please also keep in mind that nonverbal behavior, more popularly known as body language, also plays a large role in sarcasm. It is important for parents to watch eye rolls, long sighs, scoffs, and tones of voice when communicating with their kids. If you slip down into a sarcasm sinkhole, make sure you claw your way out. Like toxic labels, seething sarcasm burns hurtful marks into your child's self-esteem.

4. Freeing Yourself from Smoldering Suspicions

Trust is key to mindful parenting. Although most parents value trust and want to promote it, some undermine it by falling into "smoldering suspicions." Parents who get into this pattern tend to believe that making their child squirm is a good way to get them to learn. The biggest problem is that even if you have Sherlock Holmes on retainer, a parent laden with suspicions is likely to lead to a child full of secrets.

Anxiety and distrust fuel smoldering suspicions. Occasionally, having some doubts about what your children are up to is normal. And working through your smoldering suspicions with the strategies I will show you can be very helpful. If you find yourself, however, obsessing about trusting your child to the point that you can't focus on anything else, or you can't sleep, then consult a trained mental health professional. And keep this in mind: Even if your worst fears come true—that your child is using drugs, sexually active, or about to fail the school year—there is always hope. Life goes on, and so will both of you. Whatever trouble your child is involved in can spur more openness in the future. The most important thing you can do as a parent is stay involved, and you are—otherwise, you would not be reading this book. The more you lead with understanding and support, the more open your child will be with you.

Parents with smoldering suspicions tend to be anxious and need to believe that they are in control. This leads to a vicious cycle: The more anxiety a parent struggles with about their child, the more trust is eroded. The benefit of the doubt gets swallowed up by the consequences of suspicion.

Andre, age eight, was not the most graceful child. However, despite Jack, Andre's dad, making Andre the prime suspect, he did not break the picture frame in the living room. Jack fell prey to smoldering suspicions. He did not realize that the picture frame had been blown over by the wind (it sat next to an open window). His wife had forgotten to tell him about the mishap when it happened a few days earlier. Jack learned of his erroneous conclusion and vowed to be less suspicious. Sadly, smoldering suspicions can crack relationships more deeply than could ever be justified by a picture frame.

In another case, Allen found a lighter in the car of his sixteen-year-old son, Tim. Almost rivaling the "dog ate my homework" excuse, this lighter had actually fallen out of his friend Steve's pocket. As hard as it was to believe, Tim did not even know the lighter was in his own car. When his father wrongfully accused him of smoking cigarettes, the situation became ugly very quickly. Fortunately, Allen apologized for his erroneous inferential leap, and the conflict was worked out.

The tragic truth is that parents prone to smoldering suspicions create a child-fulfilling prophesy. Their distrust leads them only to further difficulty with trusting their children. When a parent feels that their child is avoidant, toxic thoughts involving smoldering suspicions are easily triggered. And their anxiety leads them to jump to conclusions.

Healthy and open communication is the best tool any parent has to stay connected to a child. As children approach their teen years, they often learn how to become even more elusive. However, as teens grapple with the conflicting urges to please their parents and their peers (never mind themselves), treating your teen with suspicion is counterproductive.

Evidence is truly critical for overcoming smoldering suspicions. The more out of control a parent believes her child to be, the more controlling she becomes in her thoughts—often by using faulty, distorted, accusatory explanations to fill in the blanks. The best way to counter smoldering suspicions is to get evidence based in reality. Reality is the antidote to all anxious, irrational thoughts, such as "She is obviously up to no good," "I just can't trust him," or "I'm scared I will never get the real story of what is going on." Often, you will be able to do this on your own by simply looking at the facts and repeatedly reminding yourself of them. For example, Joan, the mother of fifteen-year-old Gloria, had the smoldering suspicion that Gloria was getting high with friends when she did not respond to Joan's phone calls. Joan centered her thinking by realizing that:

- Gloria has been open with me about the temptations some of her friends have thrown her way.
- Gloria swore to me that she would never get in a car with anyone if they were drunk or high.
- Being overly suspicious is counterproductive for building trust with Gloria.
- The more I focus on catching Gloria being truthful instead of being deceitful, the more we will trust each other.

The cycle of suspicion becomes more entrenched when your child seizes up with smoldering suspicions toward you. Your child may think, "You're psycho. You must be going through my room! You talk about my earning your trust, but I can't even trust you."

When it comes to parenting, or any relationship for that matter, honesty is usually the best policy. My advice is to detoxify your suspicious thoughts as much as you can on your own and then share them with your child. But be sure to avoid an accusatory tone! If you can approach the subject in a positive and honest way, you have a much better chance of getting a positive response from your child.

Once Joan detoxified, she was able to honestly state her parenting dilemma to Gloria: "I really love you and want us to be open with each other. I'm feeling concerned about your new group of friends. I don't want you to feel I am punishing you for being open with me. It is just that sometimes I get really worried about you, and my head fills with doubts about your not being safe. I'm asking if you can hear me without getting so angry and accept that I am working on it. How can we meet each other halfway in my getting some piece of mind that you are safe and your getting more privacy and independence?" I never met a child or teen who did not welcome this type of openness and acceptance from her parents. Keep detoxifying, and the solutions will emerge. Remember, good parenting is about calming down and problem solving. Table 6.6 provides more ways to get rid of smoldering suspicions.

Table 6.6 More ways to douse smoldering suspicion

Toxic Thoughts	Evidence to the Contrary	Alternative Thoughts
"You did not even watch your brother while I was gone."	"Many times you have been responsible for your brother."	"It is best that I keep time intervals of babysitting shorter so I don't get so suspicious. This will avoid setting the stage for disappointment. Then I can praise success."
"He sleeps so much lately, he must be doing drugs."	"He does go to his job, and he does have this persistent springtime allergy problem."	"He may also be feeling down or even depressed with all the school stress he is under. I am going to try more listening than lecturing."
"She is lying that she does not have homework. I can't trust her at all."	"She has lied about homework, but that does not mean she really does not care about her future. She is just stuck right now."	"I will remind myself that the school issues have been going on for some time. I hope to have the school psychologist test her to help determine what is at the heart of the problem."

I am not asking parents to be blindly naive. As you will soon see, when I talk about "detrimental denial," this is not the answer. Children and teens can certainly dupe parents. In the privacy of my office, children have shared many secrets with me. I continue to be amazed at how determined kids can outwit their parents. As I mentioned earlier, I have learned of secret marijuana apparatuses stored in floor vents and drop ceilings, secret outings with the car into the night, stolen money, sexual acting out, and many other escapades. Smoldering suspicions, however, only fuel the deceit. The best way to undo the damage is to build trust. Building trust may take time, but it works far better at getting the truth than suspicion and hypervigilant attempts to control children.

5. Digging Out of Detrimental Denial

Detrimental denial is different from all the other toxic thoughts. The other eight reflect parents' struggling with rigid, critical thoughts about their children. Detrimental denial, however, is the polar opposite of smoldering suspicions. Parents with detrimental denial avoid taking responsibility for their child's concerns and problems. Instead of helping to find solutions, they rigidly make excuses for their child's issues.

Parents with detrimental denial are terrified to appear less than perfect as parents. I have heard some very sad stories of parents who have had troubling and even tragic wake-up calls. It is hard to maintain denial, for example, when your child is caught on videotape stealing from a store. Learning that your child was caught cheating in school can also be upsetting. Children can also trespass, bully others, and be reckless. And, in the extreme, parents may even get a dreaded call in the middle of the night and hear that their child has been seriously injured or has died in an accident.

I had an extreme situation in my practice years ago in which a sixteen-year-old boy had exploded with rage and almost ran his parents over with the car when they tried to block him from leaving. Fortunately, no one was hurt. As I sat with him and his parents, trying to make sense of it all, he explained that he had been crying out for help for many years. The parents had sincerely not been able to see, or take seriously, the signals.

When I worked at a college counseling center years ago I saw an extreme case of detrimental denial. A very bright, attractive young girl, who was an Olympic-caliber gymnast, attempted suicide. Her parents came in from out of town, and in a marathon therapy session the girl shared that she never felt she measured up to her parents' expectations. The father declared that he finally understood his daughter's emotional pain. Yet out of the blue, his final words as the session ended were, "If you could only get it together, you could really soar!"

Parents in detrimental denial have lost contact, at least in part, with reality. It can be very tempting to believe that your child's problems don't exist or are the fault of his teacher, his school, his peers, or his coach. After all, if your child is not responsible and it is the other party's fault, then this absolves *you* of any fault or liability. But rarely are a child's problems exclusively the fault of others in his life.

It may feel really good or even natural to overlook your own or your child's role in his problems. Yet this strategy usually makes things worse. A seventeen-year-old client of mine said something very wise: "My mother always told me that I was smarter than the other kids. This gave me the sense that I did not have to do as much work as anyone else. It ended up giving me a false sense of security because I thought I *really was* smarter than everyone else. I can't blame my mom for my failing math this year, but her denial of my problems didn't help."

Jenny, mother of nine-year-old Liz, fell into detrimental denial about the relationship between Marty, her second husband, and her daughter. Marty had a rather punitive style of parenting that he felt had worked well years earlier with his adult children. Jenny thought that Liz was overly sensitive and should not let Marty get to her so much. When Liz started manifesting early symptoms of an eating disorder, I expressed concern that it may be related to her problems with her stepfather. I could see that Liz did not feel she had control at home, which may have caused her problems with food. In counseling, Jenny worked through her detrimental denial with the following alternatives:

- Liz has a right to her own feelings about Marty.
- Liz's need for support from her mother is not only because she is overly sensitive, and at least she is open about her needs.

Table 6.7   More alternatives to detrimental denial

Toxic Thoughts	Evidence to the Contrary	Alternative Thoughts
"His teachers are grading him way too harshly and are out to get him this year."	"His teachers did acknowledge his progress this last marking period. They simply stressed that he is still not working up to his potential."	"The good news is that his teachers have been contacting me and apprising me of their concerns. Seeing it through their eyes helps me be more responsive to him."
"If only she did not hang out with that new friend of hers. She is the real cause of her decision to smoke and get drunk."	"My daughter is not an angel. I was the one who caught her trying cigarettes last year. She did not even know this girl then."	"Her problems are not an indication that I am a bad parent. In fact, I am a better parent for seeing that my daughter needs some help."
"She would never spread rumors the way that neighbor is saying she did."	"Come to think of it, she does like to gossip even when she is in front of me."	"We will work on this gossip issue. Better to bring it out into the light and address it now than ignore it and have it become worse later on."

- Accepting a stepparent is often a challenging process for any child.
- Even if Liz and Marty have difficulties, that does not negate all of his virtues and what he has to offer as a husband and as a stepfather.

I have heard from many parents over the years who left their heads in the sand when it came to knowing their own children's issues, and it led only to frustration. The fact that you are reading this section bodes great hope for digging out of detrimental denial if you are in it. Table 6.7 has more alternatives to illustrate how you can begin to see your children more clearly.

You may be wondering, "Hey, Dr. Jeff, what about times when teachers don't treat kids fairly or specialized educational plans are not followed?" Or "What about coaches who do favor other kids?" Or "How about my kid's friends who are a bad influence on him?"

Yes, these are all real concerns and important ones. And once in a while you must protect and advocate for your child. There's no doubt about that. But providing valid intervention on behalf of your child is far different from a pattern of distortion and denial. We know that when love is blind in romantic relationships, bitter realities and disappointments tend to follow. If you have a blind eye for the child you love, you can expect a similar outcome.

Bart and James are twins. These two boys were polite and respectful to me, but they had struggled emotionally due to being caught in the middle of their parents' acrimonious divorce. Doug, their father, prided himself on being a "cool dad." In many messy divorce situations, the children's concerns fall off the radar screen. This situation was no different. Unfortunately, Bart and James made some big mistakes by selling prescription drugs and skipping school.

Doug had an addiction, of sorts, to being liked by others. Although he was in sales and quite successful at work, when it came to Bart and James, Doug sold himself a devastating denial and avoidance package. He had initially covered up for Bart and James by making excuses to the school attendance office. Unfortunately, Doug's attempts to be cool and laid-back ended up making the situation worse for his two sons who were crying out for help. Doug later realized the drawbacks of his denial. Fortunately, school discipline, probation with the county court, and community service all helped Bart and James have some long-overdue accountability.

Detrimental denial can be due to a sense of entitlement. In these cases, the parents cannot tolerate the thought that "my kid may not be perfect." In contrast, other parents with denial issues may be so overly burdened that they ignore the child's negative behaviors. Austin, age fourteen, was kicked out of a private school because he also had sold illegal prescription drugs. Patty, his mother, refused to see Austin's role in this mess. Instead, she blamed it on a wimpy school administration. Not surprisingly, Patty tried to convince me that it was my fault on two occasions when he missed scheduled sessions with me.

Some parents can be more manipulative and subtle in expressing their entitlement-fueled denial. As I mentioned in Chapter 3, this is usually indicated by an initial apology followed by a "but" and then a whole lot of blame. In a combined family I had worked with I saw a very extreme case of this manipulative behavior. The husband apologized to his wife for his fifteen-year-old son's molestation of her eleven-year-old daughter. Yet then he implied that the girl had solicited the abuse. In response to such blatant denial, the marriage dissolved, and a big legal mess ensued. Although this case is severe, it illustrates how denial can be highly insidious and damaging.

Denial often rescues children from the natural consequences of their behavior, depriving them of the opportunity to learn responsibility for their actions. These children are hindered in developing their coping skills and problem-solving abilities. I will talk more about how to handle the consequences of your child's behavior in Chapter 8. But first, in Chapter 7, I will show you how to extinguish the four flaring toxic thoughts.

To Sum It All Up

The slow-burning toxic thoughts discussed in this chapter can be quickly dealt with by challenging them with effective alternatives. Keep the following in mind:

- Alternatives are powerful tools to dispute slow-burning toxic thoughts.
- The more you tune in to your slow-burning toxic thoughts, the more you will identify them.
- Slow-burning toxic thoughts must be challenged in order to stop them from spreading and intensifying.
- Focusing on the evidence to detoxify your thoughts will help you connect more positively with your child.

Chapter 7

Extinguish "Flaring"
Toxic Thoughts

I N THIS CHAPTER I will show you how to extinguish your flaring toxic thoughts. These thoughts tend to spark quickly into explosive outbursts. Again, alternative thoughts are the antidote. Remember to apply the stress-reduction exercises and tips from Chapter 4 and the mindfulness discussion from Chapter 5 as well. Following are the alternatives for the four remaining, more incendiary toxic thoughts.

6. Cooling Down Your Emotional Overheating

Tammy was the emotional overheater I discussed in Chapter 3. She had been quite frazzled by balancing caring for her elderly father, fearing a layoff at work, and parenting Amy, her feisty fifteen year old. You already know the story of how Tammy freaked out when Amy accidentally lobbed an eyeliner at Tammy's face.

Tammy was able to cool down her overheating thoughts by coming up with sound alternative ways to think about Amy. Read on to learn how you can do the same with your child.

Emotional overheating can cause deep scars in parent-child relationships. It is laden with distortions, usually about the child's emotional stability. Parents begin to wonder, "Is there something really wrong with him?" or "Is she just too big a problem for me to handle?" Emotional overheating is explosive reactivity to your child. Parents with emotional overheating tend to be overwhelmed by the demands of parenting. They also feel guilty and deeply inadequate for their inner turmoil. Given their emotional vulnerability, it is not surprising that emotional overheaters get pounded with the other toxic thoughts. These most often include the "always or never" trap and label gluing.

Many emotional-overheating parents are filled with a sense of shame because they perceive expressing emotions as a sign of weakness. Sadly, once they feel weak, they also feel helpless and ineffective. This feeling of powerlessness leads to the explosions of anger.

Emotional overheaters are conflicted. They want both to let their children make their own mistakes and to protect them from disappointments. Unfortunately, when these parents overreact, what they say in the heat of the moment often leaves children feeling hurt and devalued.

I have also seen that emotional overheating can lead certain parents to fall into the trap of using the silent treatment on their children. These parents believe, consciously or not, that ignoring their child will teach the kid a lesson. Obviously, this strategy is passive-aggressive and quite adolescent. It is hurtful and rarely productive. As much as they are filled with strong emotions, these parents have difficulty directly expressing themselves, so their feelings (usually anger and underlying hurt or disappointment) come out in more indirect ways, such as not talking or slamming doors.

The ability to feel vulnerable flies out the window when emotional overheating occurs. As is so often the case, when Tammy, whom I discussed above, emotionally overheated, she became emotionally unavailable to Amy. This only, in turn, amplified Amy's frustrations. She could not, then, feel emotionally safe with her mother. As was the case for Tammy, the key word for those who emotionally overheat is *can't*. In one form or another, the thought is "I *can't* handle her" or "I *can't* take it."

I helped Tammy to explore her "can't handle this" mind-set and how it limited her with Amy. Tammy learned to focus on all the times that Amy was cooperative and caring. She used this evidence to rewire her own emotional responses to Amy. She learned to accept her own feelings without judging them. Hence, she was able to lose her feelings of shame. This sense of increased acceptance and patience from Tammy, in turn, empowered Amy to begin to see her mother as more emotionally available. Tammy's evidence for alternatives looked like this:

- Amy helps me out by babysitting her younger sister, and this makes life less stressful for me.
- Amy and I have some really good laughs together, and that fills my tank when I am running on empty.
- She really is empathetic to the needs of others.
- I can feel exasperated, but that does not mean I have to take it out on Amy just because she is the oldest.

If you emotionally overheat, you need to become mindful of your "can'ts." Useful alternatives to "can't" is "will try" or "having difficulty" or similar thoughts that will help you handle your child's challenges. Table 7.1 presents some ways to use alternatives to avoid overheating your emotional fuse. Use these types of alternatives and you will relate to your child in a way that is more stable and less volatile.

Emotionally overheating usually can be effectively dealt with by using the alternative thinking strategies I have shown in table 7.1. However, if you or your child has emotional reactions that are overly excessive or obsessive, like increasing fits of rage, then professional help needs to be considered. Self-mutilation, holes in the wall, and broken doors are examples that I have seen. Emotional

Table 7.1   More alternatives to emotional overheating

Toxic Thoughts	Evidence to the Contrary	Alternative Thoughts
"I can't handle his moody outbursts."	"Actually, he usually gets moody when I start nagging him."	"His teachers love him, and he really can hold it together when it counts. I am going to work on not taking him so personally."
"She is way too manipulative for me to manage her."	"I did my share of manipulating when I was her age, too. She is no different than I was, and I turned out okay."	"I am going to tactfully use some humor and call her on her manipulations. The less reactive I get, the less I will feel that she is so tough to deal with."
"She's too much to deal with."	"Actually, compared to some of her friends, she really is not so high-maintenance after all."	"Her intensity, once she learns to channel it, will probably serve her well in this competitive world. It feels good to remind myself of that, to help me calm down."

volatility like this can signal depression, anxiety, or other mental health issues that may warrant professional attention.

I shared the example of Claire and Jonathan in Chapter 3. She found herself pulling her son's hair in reaction to Jonathan's rude comments and his stubborn addiction to video games. I empathized with Claire's frustrations and helped her tune in to all of her thoughts. She also learned self-calming strategies. This helped her slow down and cool down. Then she extinguished her toxic thoughts with some alternatives. These included:

- He did start taking piano lessons this year, so he is branching out in some new directions.
- I am not a big fan of these video games, but he is inviting the new neighbor over, and they seem to enjoy playing them together.

- For most kids, these video games are a stage, and the more I remind myself of that, the less this will be such a volatile issue.
- The more I get in a power struggle over the video games, the more he will be prone to use them to rebel against me.

If not dealt with, emotional overheating happens over and over again because the parent who overheats rarely learns to accommodate his child's reactions. In reality, these reactions are not new and not truly as dark or malicious as the parent perceives. The sad aftermath of emotional overheating, however, is that the child can lose respect for and also be fearful of the parent.

For the most part, emotional overheating occurs when parents are unable to manage their stress and negative thoughts toward their children, or even life in general. Obviously, however, if you discover that your child is involved in extreme and risky behaviors, such as acting out sexually, using or dealing drugs, or committing crimes, then this is a different story, and I suggest that you consult a health care professional.

It is my hope that if you emotionally overheat, you will use alternatives to cool down. The earlier that parents learn to spot their overheating patterns and challenge them, the less screaming that will occur. Not only can emotional overheating lead to verbal tirades, but like all unchecked toxic thoughts, it can also possibly lead to physical abuse.

7. Breaking Free from Blame Blasting

I shared in Chapter 3 how Regan instigated a fight with her brother, Javon, which led their mother, Sharon, to blame Javon for ruining her plans for a calm dinner with her kids.

I am all for seeing children held accountable for their actions. But toxically blaming kids is a different story. The phrases "Your fault," "You don't," and "If only" are red flags for blame blasting. You will know that you are blame blasting if you make statements to your child like "You're ruining our dinner," "It's your fault, not mine, that you are going to fail your math class," or "If only you would stop doing this, we'd be okay."

I worked with Sharon and helped her overcome her tendencies to blame-blast Javon. In order to do this, she had to challenge her blame-blasting thought pattern. She realized that once she used the following alternatives, she no longer was a blame blaster:

- I tend to be hard on Javon to toughen him up, but the reality is that he has tried to help us be a stronger family.
- Regan does her fair share of provoking Javon.
- The more I blame Javon for family problems, the more I am creating more of them.
- Sometimes I really do need to lighten up and remember that both kids are still growing up.

I have seen children unfairly blamed for many things. It certainly makes it hard for children to develop healthy relationship skills when they are on the receiving end of blame. "You made me yell at you" or, in more extreme cases, "You made me hit you" is about as toxic an example as you can get.

In one extreme case, a defiant teenage girl I worked with had been blamed by her mother for her father's heart attack. This left an indelible mark of shame that the girl carried around inside her. Obviously, this is an extreme case, but it speaks to just how off the charts blame can get.

Parents get into blame because they are seeking an answer to the question "Who did it?" rather than "What can we do about it?". Blame communicates the desire to punish, which only shuts down the child, leading to missed opportunities to resolve the conflict.

Table 7.2   Going from blame to cooperation

Blaming and Shaming Toxic Words	Reasonable and Realistic Words
You	We
"You messed this all up."	"Let's work together to figure out what went wrong and get beyond it."
"If only you stuck with it."	"This is not working. Let's come up with a better idea."
"You don't even care."	"I know what it is like to feel stuck. My sense is that you feel this way too."
"You caused this problem, not me."	"Blaming you is a waste of time. I am asking for your help to make it better for both of us."

Going from Blame Blasting to Cooperative Listening

Check out table 7.2 to see some alternative words and phrases that will help you put down your blame battering ram. If you replace these blaming and shaming words with more cooperative words, you and your child will be in a much healthier place.

Think of the alternative words in table 7.2 as stilts lifting you up to rise above the low pettiness of blame. The less you blame your child, the more you will invite him to be accountable on his own. You may slip once in a while and start to blame-blast your child. Above all, if this happens, don't blame yourself or beat yourself up. Be empowered to see that you can overcome toxic-thought patterns. Changing how you think will change how you conduct yourself.

I am often asked, "But Dr. Jeff, what if what I'm blaming my child for is truly his fault?" I'm not saying your kid is an angel. Your child may have forgotten to do something, messed up something, overlooked something, or gotten caught up in his own world. Indeed, your child may have done something serious that requires consequences. Rest assured that in the next chapter, I will soon address the optimal ways for parents to deliver consequences for problematic behaviors in children. As you will see, the key is to not let your emotions get the best of you when trying to guide your child toward what is best for him. How you think and react is your responsibility—not his. If you stop focusing on who's to blame, then

Table 7.3   More alternatives to blame blasting toxic thought

Toxic Thoughts	Evidence to the Contrary	Alternative Thoughts
"She's the reason the younger ones are acting so anxious and moody."	"It has not been easy with her going through this rough time, but she did not choose to be born with anxiety issues and a learning disability."	"Blaming her only makes it worse. The younger ones will certainly see some unhealthy behaviors that I hope they will see are not good choices."
"He's not taking one ounce of responsibility for his school problems."	"He is trying harder now; it is just that he has gotten himself into such a big hole with school."	"It's easier when I remind myself that his getting through school is a process. My expectations may not be fair if he can't meet them."
"Your moodiness is what leaves us all feeling like hostages in this house."	"We tried counseling, and it helped for a while. Her friend's dad has cancer, and I think she is emotionally maxed out."	"We will get through this. I will set up another appointment with the counselor and see if it helps. In the meantime, I'm going to stop demanding she be nice and try being nice to her."

the focus is on the issue, and issues are much easier to work through than blame. Table 7.3 provides concrete examples of how you can gather evidence to challenge and change your thoughts of blame.

8. Stopping Your "Should" Slamming

Many parents want to teach their children valuable life lessons. As parents, we by definition have experience far beyond that of our children. And it is incumbent upon us to teach our children the ways of the world. After all, we parents want to see our kids avoid disappointments and hurts that come with mistakes.

Yet too often parents who try to pass on their wisdom end up imposing it instead. There is no better way to push beliefs on a child than to tell her what she should and shouldn't do. The biggest problem with *should*s is that they create a strong sense of shame. I call this "'should' slamming."

As I discussed in Chapter 3, "should" statements that are directed against your child, other people, or the world in general lead to anger and frustration: "He shouldn't be so stubborn and argumentative!" "Musts," "oughts," and "have tos" cause the same type of pressuring dynamic. Rigid thinking patterns like these create guilt in the child's mind if he makes mistakes or struggles.

We all know that well-meaning parents "want the best" for the children they love. The problem is that these wants often lead to *should*s. *Should*s are immature, and they disrupt communication, and harm relationships over time.

If you look back on your own childhood, at a very young age you most likely learned to associate bad feelings with the word *should*. Most every kid has heard her parent saying that she should have done or should not have done something in particular. And usually the parent is also implying that the kid is bad. We learn that when we do something that we "shouldn't" do, we are bad—and when we do not do things we "should," we are also bad.

I've got some great news for you. Simply phrasing and reframing your thoughts using alternatives such as "would like" instead of "should" will be very helpful. *Should*s reflect demanding, rigid, unrealistic expectations (especially as the other person doesn't know what we're thinking!). By saying phrases such as "would like" instead of "should," we relieve the pressure on the child.

"Should" suggests "you must," whereas "would like" suggests "let's cooperate." Effective parenting is based on cooperating, not mandating. Once Bruce, the father who sent his son to military school, understood the problems with the word *should*, he instantly knew the biggest piece of evidence against his toxic thought: He had never told Brock that he was worried about his being happy and content later in life. Simply realizing that his son couldn't read his mind and understand that "I'm worried about you and want

Table 7.4   More alternatives to "should" slamming toxic thoughts

Toxic Thoughts	Evidence to the Contrary	Alternative Thoughts
"Glen should know I don't want him talking to those kids down the street."	"He's a teenager, and it's unrealistic for me to assume he knows how I feel."	"I would like to get to know his friends better so I don't get so uptight about what he is doing. At that point I can make a less reactive judgment."
"He should share with me how he is doing in school."	"He did tell me that he is scared he is failing his science class."	"I would like for us to find a way that he can feel safer to tell me more of what is going on with him at school."
"She should be more respectful of my new boyfriend."	"She did let me know that she's very preoccupied thinking about her father moving out of state and still blames me for it."	"I will consider pacing this new relationship a little slower so she is not so overwhelmed by it."

you to be okay. Please let me help you!" enabled Bruce to create this alternative: "I *would like* it if Brock and I could talk things out so I can support him and help him make good choices."

I also recall working with Peter, a hard-driving yet well-meaning stepfather to Celia. Peter felt that Celia should accept him as a stepparent because he was very kind to her and her mother, Stacey. Once Peter stopped his *should*s, however, he realized that he was not demanding respect anymore. And that's when he began to get it.

The more that you zap *should*s from your mind, the less your child will mind talking to you. *Should*s create a demanding dynamic that children will usually push against. It will end up shutting them down. Thinking and expressing "would like" versus "should" is more likely to gain cooperation, build trust, and create a stronger parent-child bond.

I won't tell you that you *should* take my advice. I hope, however, that you will be willing to consider it.

9. Undoing Dooming Conclusions with Realistic Reasoning

"Dooming conclusions" is a toxic-thinking pattern in which parents exaggerate the negative actions and events concerning their children. They are unfair, exaggerated negative predictions. These fatalistic conclusions block parents and children from working out problems together.

One of the unfair ironies of dooming conclusions is that they can lead not only to a breakdown of trust and communication but also to the very event feared by the parent. As I said in Chapter 2, what we dwell on is what we are prone to see. When parents focus on what they don't want their children to do, their children become more inclined to do just that.

Thoughts like "I have so much on my plate, and now I have to learn this. Why can't he simply do what he has to do to get through life?" can permeate any area of the child's life, including school ("He's going to fail out and be on the streets"), peers ("She will never make any friends"), or home ("I can't ever see us having sanity in this house because of her antics"). Dooming conclusions unfairly lower your ability to believe in your child. This is tragic, because your disbelief leaves your child feeling disempowered.

Stressed-out parents prone to anxiety are particularly at risk of forming dooming conclusions, as are parents who have unresolved "emotional ghosts." For example, dooming conclusions smothered the thinking of Jan. She was very concerned that the obesity genes in her family would grab hold of her preteen daughter, Sylvia. Jan was an exercise fanatic, and she was frustrated that Sylvia did not respond when prodded to exercise. Sylvia was at times receptive, but not as enthusiastic as Jan wanted her to be. Sylvia, like many pubertal girls, was slightly overweight, and had recently begun overeating, in part, as she confided in me, to rebel against her mother. Fortunately, Jan saw me for some separate counseling and became less catastrophic in picturing her daughter's future. This also helped Jan pressure her daughter less.

Sylvia gradually began to adapt her own healthy lifestyle of nutrition and exercise.

The way to zap dooming conclusions is to challenge them with alternative evidence. In the following list, you will see by way of Jan as an example how these gloomy, unfair forecasts of a child's future failure can be challenged. As part of her own counseling, Jan confronted her fear of Sylvia's becoming obese by grounding herself in the facts:

- Jan educated Sylvia about food in ways that her own parents had never educated her.
- Sylvia had recently taken an increased interest in her own health and appearance.
- Many girls can be overweight when younger and slim down after puberty.
- Even if Sylvia had a propensity for weight-related concerns, she could still find joy in her life.

Jan was able to review the evidence and tell herself, "Sylvia has a right to live her own life. I can educate her about making healthy choices with food. At the same time, I don't want to give her the message that she is bad if she struggles with her eating and her weight. The more I keep my message consistent but less intrusive, the more she will likely listen to me."

Jan and Sylvia's story teaches us a powerful lesson: By identifying and disputing dooming conclusions, you can turn them into optimistic opportunities. Table 7.5 gives further examples of alternatives to dooming conclusions as they apply to other situations.

Also, as one more strategy, remember that seven-word magical question I discussed in Chapter 4: "What's the worst thing that can happen?" More often than not, that question can put concerns in a more realistic, healthy perspective. So you can always ask that

Table 7.5 More alternatives to dooming conclusions

Toxic Thoughts	Evidence to the Contrary	Alternative Thoughts
"Her lying so often at this age will lead to her being messed up and in constant trouble later on."	"She does admit to me things she struggles with. It is when I start to yell that she reacts by telling me what I want to hear."	"All children go through stages, to varying degrees, where they tell tales or shade the truth. It is unfair of me to impose my fears of this never tapering off. The more I praise her for telling the truth, the more likely she will continue to do so."
"He is never going to be able to sit still and keep quiet. He probably has ADHD and is in store for a challenging life."	"This has been a rough year for him with my going back to work. He actually is relatively less hyper and impulsive than when we first moved."	"Even if it does turn out that he has ADHD, there is no reason to panic. We can always get him evaluated and treated, if needed. Let me see how he does the rest of the year."
"She is going to be promiscuous and lose all of the sense of morality we tried to instill in her."	"Just because she started hanging out with this new crowd does not mean we lost her for life. She even told me how she does not want to become involved in meaningless sex."	"I have a right to be concerned, but going overboard with worry won't help matters. The best thing I can do is be here for her to share and talk without her feeling like I don't like her for who she is."

question to get a reality check. Obviously, if your child is in immediate risk of harm to herself or others, then outside professional care is warranted.

Now That You Are Detoxified

Congratulations. You now have learned how to detoxify the thoughts that get in the way of liking the child you love. You may wonder, "How long do I have to do this work?" It's true that gathering evidence and developing alternatives are work. But what a good cause this is! As you detoxify your thinking and your behaviors, you will build up more understanding and connection with your child. Remember, as you go forward, "It is easier to build a child than to repair an adult."

And guess what? You won't have to do this work so intensively forever. Just as your toxic thoughts were once automatic, your better way of thinking will become automatic, too. Soon you will be able to dispute your toxic thoughts in an instant. It takes only a little time, practice, and patience.

To Sum It All Up

The freedom to choose your thoughts is a wonderful gift for both you and your child. Using the tools in this chapter, you are now empowered to gather evidence to dispute and counter your toxic thinking and develop better, healthier alternatives. Keep the following in mind:

- It is surprisingly easy to detoxify your toxic thoughts.
- Flaring toxic thoughts can be extinguished with alternatives.
- Focusing on the evidence to detoxify your thoughts will help you see previously overlooked positive behaviors in your child.
- The less toxic you think, the less toxic you will act.
- Your child will favorably respond to your detoxifying your thoughts.

Chapter 8

Dependable Discipline:
Lessening the Consequences
to Gain Control

L ILLIAN WAS LIVID. She was completely stumped on how to get her thirteen-year-old son, Zach, to wear a helmet when he was skateboarding. "Okay, Dr. Jeff, so now what?" she asked. "I took your advice and really worked on getting rid of my toxic thoughts. I also have been more calm and less controlling—I've tried really hard. But Dr. Jeff, there are times like this when I want to lay down the law and take everything away from him when he does not listen. I really feel I need to step in and show him who is boss!"

Lillian had major PFS, as Zach's refusal to wear a helmet could lead to a dangerous situation. Lillian had every right to want her son to wear a helmet. It was understandable that she was upset, although being upset was not productive.

Like most parents trying to get their kids to do something important, Lillian threatened Zach with Big Consequences. Of course, you may say—why wouldn't and shouldn't Lillian speed down the Consequence-City Expressway with Zach? Well, the biggest reason is because too often when parents rush in with consequences, they end up crashing and burning.

Taking a step back, I asked Lillian to further describe what had been going on with her son. She shared countless stories of power

165

struggles with Zach over his lack of helmet compliance. She had taken the skateboard away for a day and then a week. Oh, sure, when, after relentlessly pestering his mother, Zach got the skateboard back, he would *then* don the helmet. But this was only temporary, soon followed by his removing the helmet immediately.

As Lillian reflected on her attempts to discipline Zach, she felt very confused. Why was it that Zach's helmet compliance did not get better with the consequences? Lillian decided to prolong keeping away the skateboard, but she grew even more frustrated when she spied Zach using a friend's board. Yelling, pleading, and even revoking other things, like Zach's computer or phone privileges, all fell short.

Lillian was upset that Zach did not seem to understand her reasoning. "Why is this so difficult?" she agonized. "Plain and simple: No helmet, no skateboard." Yet taking things away from Zach did not end up taking away the problem. No matter what she seemed to do, Zach was still using his skateboard (or those of friends) without wearing a helmet! Needless to say, the situation became a major power struggle every time she took away the skateboard, or anything else for that matter. Screaming, tears, and a broken dish were among the aftermath.

Filled with toxic thoughts to the hilt, Lillian was exasperated. As with so many parents, she found it difficult to like her child when he did not like listening to her. Complicating matters was that Lillian also knew that she liked, and for that matter loved, the idea of consequences. Many parents feel this way. After all, who wants to be a wimpy parent and let their kids blatantly disobey? And won't consequences help your kids learn right from wrong? Very good questions. Yet what beguiled Lillian to no end was her realization that imposing consequences on Zach did not help. Actually, they only made the situation worse.

So how did this helmet-resistant son and mother work it out? First, Lillian sat down, and she and Zach had a good old-fashioned "meeting of the minds." But this time she did it differently—she decided to use her ears more than her mouth. Lillian made a commitment to learn how imposing consequences on her son was getting in the way of understanding him. She sat down with Zach and probed *why* he didn't wear the helmet. She realized, as he spoke, that there was more than one reason and more than one solution:

- Zach expressed that his helmet did not fit right. He then agreed to go with Lillian to pick out a more comfortable one.
- The helmet had been residing on the top shelf of Zach's closet, and this led to "out of sight and out of mind." They both agreed to keep it on a shelf in the laundry room, which adjoined the garage where he kept his skateboard. It was much harder to miss when put in a prominent place.
- Zach also admitted what Lillian really feared: He felt that the helmet was "uncool." Lillian, however, had done her homework and calmly reinforced how most pro skateboarders wore helmets. To help influence and inspire her son, Lillian went with Zach to pick out a poster of his favorite skateboarder in which he was wearing a helmet.

Lillian had wisely involved Zach in finding solutions to the problem. She was committed to understanding why Zach had not been wearing the helmet. They were making progress. Yes, there were still a few instances when Zach went on the board without a helmet, but these became rare. When this occurred, Lillian kept her "emotional overheating" thoughts in check and did not yell. She simply gave a calm reminder, and twice in the next six months she had to temporarily withhold the skateboard. But the amazing part was that the meltdowns were gone. Zach was more open to Lillian's discipline because it did not feel like punishment that he needed to rebel against.

As seen in the case of Lillian and Zach, most children will not change their behavior until the underlying feeling or need has been addressed and a solution found. This is so important to bear in mind. Liking your child involves helping him like himself and his options too. The more you seek to understand your child, the more he will be in a place to connect with you and make good choices as well.

In *10 Days to a Less Defiant Child,* I describe my approach to discipline. Essentially, dependable discipline is based on a calm and collaborative mind-set that conveys love and guidance rather than "Do what I say or else." I have very often seen that when parents impose consequences, they end up creating more conflict, and there is consequently (no pun intended) further acting out by the child. That being said, there are certainly some times that consequences are warranted (see "Dependable Discipline Guidelines: How to Use Collaborative Logical Consequences Appropriately," below). I really do agree that teaching your child what you will and won't accept is important. At the same time, it's equally important to help children learn how to take responsibility for their actions, to learn from their actions, and to relate openly and positively to others.

How Controlling Your Toxic Thoughts Helps You Discipline

A valuable by-product of getting your toxic thoughts under control is that your relationship with your child will be stronger. A strong parent-child relationship usually corresponds to more compliant kids. This leads to less conflict, and fewer consequences will be needed. At the same time, kids being kids, they will test your limits. For most parents, setting limits can be quite challenging. Parents tend to get upset in the process. So when you do use consequences, administering them while in control of your toxic thoughts will keep your emotionality in check. The more calm and firm you are, the more your child will comply.

I can't emphasize enough, however, that it really pays to be judicious and put some thought into how and why you might use consequences. If you overuse negative consequences or use them inconsistently, they can backfire with surprising and unwanted repercussions.

Why Consequences Can Be Combustible

Many children, particularly those prone to defiant behavior, will react adversely to consequences. When defiant children feel overly controlled and pressured, they tend to think even more distortedly. Your child reasons that he did nothing wrong and that any consequences are not fair. Thinking that he is your equal, he lashes out while thinking or saying something like, "You are making my life miserable, so I will do the same to you." Or he may reason, "See? This is what you get for making me the one in trouble."

Defiant children may also learn to avoid punishment by hiding their misbehavior from you or other authority figures. Complicating matters, if you overdo the consequences, you may end up feeling excessively guilty. And consequences often leave kids feeling a sense of shame as well, damaging their self-esteem. This will actually increase the likelihood of continued misbehavior.

As you gain control over your thoughts and speak less toxically to your kids, they will likely follow the lead and think and act less toxically too. Less toxicity will pave the way to a smoother connection. It is important to let these new, improved parent-child dynamics work for both of you.

Bypassing Your Child's Emotional Reactivity

When your child kicks up clouds of defiance, consequences are particularly prone to fail. This is because children who are defiant are acting emotionally and immaturely. They are flooded with negative thoughts and emotions. Take a look at the following list to see some of the "hot thoughts" your child may have that get in the way of her reacting constructively to imposed consequences:

Know Your Child's "Hot Thoughts"

- "I hate you [this, him, it]."
- "You are never fair."
- "No one ever listens to me."
- "You are ruining my life."
- "You're mean."
- "Why should I try to do it? You will just criticize me anyway."
- "You always blame me."
- "You always make me do this."
- "You don't care how I feel."
- "This stinks."

Do these "hot thoughts" sound a little too familiar? Now that you are this far in the program, I hope these thoughts are your child's and not yours. As you can see, upset children can have their own toxic thoughts. Rigidly applying consequences to a child flooded with such troubled thoughts is usually a setup for more problems. I recommend you read *Freeing Your Child from Negative Thinking* by Tamar Chansky for more on the subject of directly addressing your child's negative-thinking patterns.

For too many parents, too often, consequences are presented as punishments. But a punishment mentality only breaks apart, rather than builds up, mutual understanding and cooperation. Punishment means presenting a negative consequence and often has a shaming "I'm right, you're wrong" quality about it. Punishment usually increases your child's emotional reactivity, whether it's aggressive or passive-aggressive.

Effective discipline, on the other hand, emphasizes the process of teaching your child. Discipline has a "Let's work this out together" mind-set, which helps bypass your child's emotional reactivity.

Since defiant children tend to see themselves as your equal, they rebel against punishment. If your child does not regret or even acknowledge his actions, he will direct his anger at the one who inflicts the consequences, or, as he sees it, punishment—you.

The Calm, Firm, and Noncontrolling Approach

Keeping your own self-discipline is crucial for bypassing your child's emotional reactivity and effectively disciplining your child. In *10 Days to a Less Defiant Child*, I emphasized that parents who are calm, firm, and noncontrolling will bypass this emotional reactivity. Now that you have learned how to control and stay free of your toxic thoughts, you will be even more able to do this. You will not sink into the emotional quicksand of reactive punishment.

You may be wondering, "I can be calm and firm, but how can I give consequences and still be noncontrolling?" As you will see later in this chapter, it is all in your delivery. A collaborative rather than adversarial mind-set is of utmost importance.

Keep in mind that consequences alone, no matter how you present them, won't teach your child the values and skills that are important for self-worth, problem solving, and self-control. Although consequences can be helpful, the key is to understand where your child is coming from and why he is doing what he is doing in the first place. Lillian, whom I discussed at the beginning of this chapter, was eventually able to avoid power struggles with Zach over helmet compliance by being understanding, calm, firm, and noncontrolling. Although she occasionally still had to use consequences, because they were less frequent and delivered in a calm manner, they became much more effective.

Now let's discuss consequences more closely by identifying two types. These are natural and collaborative logical consequences. For children who are increasingly defiant, both types of consequences can help reduce acting out behaviors.

Natural Consequences

Natural consequences basically follow the logic of "Let the chips fall where they may." For example, if your child refuses to put on a coat, let her get cold. If your child won't eat, let her feel hungry. If she doesn't complete her homework, let her fail the assignment. If he is rude to a referee in a soccer game, let him get ejected. These are important but hard lessons, and you can count on life to be a great teacher.

Years ago, as a teenager, I got my first speeding ticket. At the time my dad shared this valuable pearl of wisdom: "Jeff, if you want to dance, then you have to pay the fiddler." What he meant was that I needed to experience the results of my bad choice so that I could learn that my actions had consequences. I did not like paying the fine, yet it helped me learn to take responsibility.

I believe that sooner or later, the world humbles all of us with natural consequences. Children may have to learn some things the hard way, but that is part of life. I recall a thirteen-year-old boy bragging to me that he stole a hairbrush at a local supermarket. Feeling a bit slick, he stole, not surprisingly, something else a few weeks later. This time he was caught, and he ended up doing some community service at a local church. In this situation, natural consequences helped him to be accountable, and he learned his lesson.

There are times, however, when parents need to intervene to protect children from the natural consequences. The consequence of dangerous behavior could be serious injury (like if Zach continued to not wear his helmet and broke his head open when skateboarding). Similarly, educational failure can be the consequence of persistently avoiding schoolwork. In this case, parents need to step in with some consequences and work closely with the school before that catastrophic natural one. As another example, a child caught stealing money from his parents may then have to do some projects around the house to make up for his transgression.

Now let's look at how parents can most effectively deliver consequences. Given how important it is for parents to stay collaborative in their mind-set, I call these "collaborative logical consequences."

Collaborative Logical Consequences

Logical consequence is a term commonly found in parenting literature to describe when parents give a consequence to a child that is related to the behavior they wish to discourage. I believe that natural consequences, when applicable, are the most effective because the child can directly see what will happen if he makes a mistake. At times, however, parents may need to step in and give a logical consequence if they feel it is warranted. For example, a child who gets rambunctious and spills his drink is told to wipe it up. If your daughter leaves her bike in the driveway and refuses to put it away after a few requests, you may put it away for her until the next day. Or in the case of that ever-challenging sibling rivalry, a toy that is being incessantly fought over is put away for ten minutes. Please see the box ("Dependable Discipline Guidelines: How to Use Collaborative Logical Consequences Appropriately") for guidelines on how to make this judgment.

In all cases where parents deliver the consequences, I suggest that the term *logical consequence* be modified to *collaborative logical consequence*. This approach emphasizes to your child that you are on his side versus becoming his adversary. Even if your child is not receptive to the consequence, which he likely won't be, it is important that *you* have a collaborative mind-set as you discuss your concern and impose the consequence.

Staying Collaborative Even If Your Child Isn't

To keep a collaborative spirit amid your child's mumbling and grumbling, it pays to implement consequences calmly and in a neutral tone. I have even acknowledged to my own children that I may want to yell and even "lose it." By disclosing this, I am defusing my own "emotional-overheating bomb arsenal." This also helps me model the ability to tune in to my own thoughts and behaviors and think before I act. However, if you deliver consequences in an emotional, dictatorial manner, your child will be less likely to be open to learning from his mistakes. Remember, you don't have to let your child's lack of enthusiasm for your newfound calm, firm, and noncontrolling approach impact you. At the same time, if you point out that you are taking action because you feel it is best for him, and do it authentically, then you won't likely fuel your child's objection.

Keep in mind that collaborative logical consequences, presented in a caring, cooperative manner, do not require the cooperation of your child. If Joey continues to play video games and refuses to do his homework, Mom and Dad, in a calm, firm, and noncontrolling manner, may have to take away the video game and lock it up. If your child breaks the rule about where he can go on his bike, you may have to take away the bike for a few days and leave it with a relative. When your child does not do her chores, and you have addressed it more than once in a calm, firm, and noncontrolling manner, then you need to take away her privilege to spend the night with a friend or rent a movie. In all these cases, the parent delivers the consequence with a collaborative attitude.

Collaborative words follow from a collaborative mind-set. For example, the parent of the child excessively playing video games may say, "I realize you don't feel good about this, but I have decided to take away your video game privilege for the rest of the night. I am hoping you get your work done so I can give the game back to you tomorrow afternoon." Giving collaborative logical consequences for misbehavior, if presented selectively and nonaggressively, can help your child learn that he is accountable for his actions. Most important, when you keep your emotion out of the consequences, your child will not feel attacked, nor will you damage his self-esteem.

I have seen countless parents give consequences, like Lillian's first unsuccessful attempts to discipline Zach, which lacked this collaborative mind-set. Then these parents fail to learn why their children's problematic behavior occurred in the first place. Consequences imposed without understanding the underlying issue will usually not be effective. The bottom line is that you need to give careful thought to the use of collaborative logical consequences with your defiant child. See the box for some guidance:

Dependable Discipline Guidelines: How to Use Collaborative Logical Consequences Appropriately

It's not always easy for parents to know whether to give consequences for misbehavior, and, if so, which ones to give. Following is a series of guidelines aimed at helping you determine when and if you should use consequences with your child:

- Are your expectations realistic? Can your child really do what you expect here? Sometimes as parents we lose perspective on our children. If your expectations are unrealistic given your child's age or emotional maturity, then consequences are not needed. If you are not being fair, change your expectations and don't give consequences.
- Did your child know at the time that she was doing something wrong? If not, explain why it was wrong but don't give consequences. Help her understand what you expect, why, and how she can accomplish it. Offer to help her.
- If your child knew what she was doing was wrong, deliberately disregarded reasonable expectations, and continues to show no interest in accepting responsibility for problem behavior, then I suggest using consequences. Discuss the concerns with your child in a calm, firm, and noncontrolling

manner, and then include the child in determining the consequences together, if at all possible.

• Did your child break a rule you both agreed on? Are you
  burned out or tired and overreacting, or is there a real
  problem here? Are you looking at the situation fairly? If
  your child did not break a known rule, then consequences
  are not needed.

••

I have so far discussed both natural and collaborative logical
consequences. Following are points to keep in mind when you give
collaborative logical consequences. These will help you implement
them successfully.

Eight More Important Points About Collaborative Logical Consequences

1. More mutual understanding leads to fewer consequences.
It is important to remember that if your child clearly understands
what is expected of him and you regularly encourage him when he
behaves well, he will be less likely to take actions that require consequences. You have likely seen that your child will work hardest
in school for teachers who he feels understand him. Similarly, he
will also be most compliant with you if you too provide that sense
of understanding.

Fueled by PFS, Jill had a Big Consequences mentality, which
led to power struggles with her nine-year-old daughter, Cynthia. Jill
had been hooked on giving Cynthia consequences for not picking
up her room. Both Jill and Cynthia were very upset at the resulting conflicts. Jill, despite being skeptical of the power of understanding, learned to change her tone. She began to acknowledge
that Cynthia felt overwhelmed and needed a "jump start" to help
clean her room. Although Cynthia's room was never quite ready
for a home-magazine photo shoot, it was in much better condition

once this mother and daughter worked as a team. Jill's newfound understanding and cooperative attitude influenced Cynthia's increased compliance.

2. Consistency and follow-through lead to better consequences. While I was an undergraduate student more than twenty-five years ago, I briefly met the noted psychologist Dr. B. F. Skinner at a professional conference. I was quite awed by him. Dr. Skinner's work showed that when we are uncertain whether we'll get a reward or what it may be, we go after our goal with serious enthusiasm. Think about it: A kid in the grocery store sees the candy and begs his mom for some. She tells him, "No, and stop bugging me or you will not get to go outside when we get home." If the child continues pleading and his mother finally feels worn down and gives in and the child is still allowed to go outside, then she is teaching the child that if he nags, he will receive only the *threat* of a consequence. Thus, he is encouraged to repeat this behavior over and over.

As you can see, consistency is important. If you give an "if, then" statement, you must follow through with the "then" part. Many parents complain to me that they are simply too tired to follow up on their "thens." We have all been there and fallen into this trap. Just remember, though, that dependable discipline relies on consistency. And the more consistent you are, the more you will conserve your energy in the long run because you'll be putting a stop to the misbehavior.

Hal told his eight-year-old son, Ian, "If you keep leaving your backpack in the middle of the floor, I will ask you to straighten up the whole mudroom." About a week later Hal almost broke his leg when he tripped on the backpack. Ian laughed at his dad's unintended display of slapstick humor. Hal, however, staying calm, stuck to his guns and had Ian clean up the mudroom. Ian then realized the joke was over. Whereas in the past Ian would wait for Hal to forget about the discipline, this time it did not work.

This all being said, realize also that it is very confusing for children if something they do earns a negative consequence today but it did not do so yesterday. Finally, it is important that negative consequences are applied to all children in the family. Even very young children will be upset if they see other children being treated differently.

3. Focusing on solutions will keep down your toxic-thought triggers. Make sure that the consequences are solution focused rather than pain focused. Think of the behavior or issue at hand. Remember that everyone makes mistakes. Try not to make it personal—instead of talking to your "bad child" (remember, no more label gluing), talk about your child's behavior. Getting very angry is not productive. In the eyes of your child, when you get angry you can be rather entertaining, either scary or exciting. This only distracts them from learning in response to the situation.

4. Brief is best. The advantage to keeping a consequence short is that you quickly give your child an opportunity to try again. For example, if the television is turned off for ten minutes because children are fighting over it, they will quickly have another opportunity to solve the problem in a different way. Too often a parent with PFS will reach for the elephant gun. The problem is that if the parent decides the TV is to stay turned off for the rest of the day, there are no more opportunities that day for them to learn to manage the situation differently. Also, a long consequence can be worse for parents than children—a child deprived of his bike or video game for a week may get bored and cranky! Remember, the consequence works best to guide and teach rather than punish.

5. Be proactive to be collaborative. Wherever possible, explain consequences to your child ahead of time so they don't come as a surprise. If you warn your child about the possible consequences of a behavior, then he is less likely to be resentful and angry when they are implemented. This helps bypass your child's emotional reactivity.

Negotiating consequences ahead of time makes them more effective and easier to implement. Involve your children as much as possible in making family rules, and help your child understand the rules and what happens when they are broken. Rules and consequences must be clear to both you and your child—I suggest putting them in writing before conflicts occur so there will be no debate over what will happen while you're in the heat of the moment. Be willing to warn your children before you implement the consequence. For example, "Guys, this yelling is too loud for me! If you can't work out what to watch on television without screaming at each other, I will turn it off for ten minutes. Please help me not have to resort to this."

6. *Timeliness is important*. Collaborative logical consequences work best when they occur as soon as possible after the misbehavior. The "wait till your father gets home!" school of discipline usually is not effective. This is because kids stressed out over delayed consequences have more time to rev up. Then they become more likely to deny responsibility for their actions. Also, they usually become angrier as time goes by. Defiant children especially are very likely to associate the consequence with the parent who's giving it rather than with their earlier misbehavior. Immediate responses are much more effective.

Betty, the mother of eight-year-old Kelly, learned the hard way why delayed consequences don't work. She told me, "Before I started working with you, I used to think I would *really* get Kelly's attention by making her reflect all day on what she did wrong if I told her she would be punished later. But I realize now that this just got her all worried and angry."

On the other hand, it may be best not to impose a consequence immediately if you are feeling very angry. There is a danger that you might overreact and be too harsh. Instead, say something like, "I am feeling very angry at the moment. We will talk about this again in a couple of minutes when I am feeling calmer."

7. *Use consequences that make sense.* Remember that the goal of solid discipline is to teach. You'd be surprised how easy it is for parents to forget that children cannot learn from consequences if they do not know that what they did was wrong. So before you respond with "trigger-happy" consequences, ask yourself, "Is my child aware that he has done something wrong, and does he understand the extent to which it creates a problem?"

Nick was a father I worked with who would reach for the consequence elephant gun for small problems. One day Nick found himself stricken with a PFS flare-up when his twin eight-year-old daughters were exuberantly bouncing and singing on his bed. "These girls are out of control!" he said to himself. "They can never just play quietly, and they always have to be so darn challenging." When Nick then threatened to not take them to see the movie he had promised earlier, Lydia, one of his daughters, said, "Dad, we're just trying to have fun." Nick reflected on these words and instantly had a flash of insight that he was not born at the age of forty-five. So he relented and said, "Okay, but please tone it down and be careful."

Well, soon after Nick's fatherly admonition, his two daughters resumed their bed bouncing with renewed vigor. Nick then heard a loud clanging sound as part of his bed frame fell to the floor. Izzy, the other twin, let out a loud shriek. This time, Nick calmly yet firmly told the girls that they would have to miss the upcoming movie. He then gave them the option of making the later afternoon show as long as they helped him make his bed, straightened up their own rooms, and shared why the bed bouncing was not such a good idea after all. Nick felt good about how he handled things. He made his point and instilled a consequence (helping him and cleaning their own rooms), yet he was noncontrolling be-

cause the girls were given the choice of missing the movie or com-
plying with the consequence.

The wonderful benefit of staying calm, firm, and noncontrolling
is that it slows you down, bypasses overreactivity, and encourages
you to pick out more sensible, effective consequences. This keeps
your child aware of what actions he did in the first place rather than
focusing on your overreactions, which he may rebel against.

8. Be willing to negotiate. Though we all need to learn accountability, there is usually still room to make amends and try to
earn back what we lose by our mistakes. Our legal system, for example, gives lawbreakers who have a cooperative attitude a break
and makes deals if they promise or exhibit better behavior. Heck,
several years ago, I even went to court to discuss one of my speeding tickets with the judge and police officer. They were impressed
with my honesty about what I did wrong and lessened the fine.

I recall working with Cole, the dad of nine-year-old Roger. Cole
was working hard to be less of a "hothead" (his self-declared label,
not mine). But one night, when Cole announced that he was taking Roger and his younger brother to a restaurant for dinner, Roger
threw a fit. "We always go where he wants, and you never care
about what I want," he said. Cole had to take a step back and
detoxify his "'should' slamming" thought: "YOU should be happy I
feed you, let alone take you to a restaurant!" Cole then used his
most calm and firm words to say that he did not appreciate Roger's
angry outburst. Roger continued to escalate, and then he threw his
brother's handheld video game down and smashed it with his feet,
cracking the plastic casing.

Cole decided that Roger needed some consequences. Though
not easy, he stayed calm, firm, and noncontrolling and told Roger
that breaking his brother's game was unacceptable. Cole firmly informed Roger that he would lose his own video game privilege for
a week. When Roger protested, Cole asked him if he was willing

to take some other actions to help reduce the time of lost video game usage. Roger agreed to apologize to his brother and do added chores to help pay for replacing his brother's broken game. Cole was still making Roger pay the consequences for his actions, but by being flexible and negotiating the consequences, he taught Roger some important accountability. Remember that discipline is much more about teaching than revenge.

Bearing in mind these eight additional points about collaborative logical consequences, take a look at the following where I provide concrete examples of dialogue showing the dependable-discipline approach:

A Contrast of Ineffective and Dependable Discipline

Most parents deliver consequences in a heated, emotional manner. This is ineffective discipline. Below are examples of toxic thoughts (TT) that lead to ineffective discipline (ID) contrasted with a more positive and rational approach, dependable discipline (DD). You will immediately see the difference.

TT: "This child is pathetic. All he does is sleep. He never takes responsibility for anything. He doesn't care at all about his life or what happens to him."

ID: "For the second time in two weeks now, you did not get up for school on time and missed the bus. You are grounded this whole weekend!"

DD: *"I am not sure what is going on with your oversleeping. I'm getting concerned and would like to discuss it tonight. We will need to look at how you can get to sleep earlier. Let's figure out how to solve this. I have some ideas, but I'd like to hear yours, too."*

TT: "Every single time I give this kid an inch, he takes a mile. You are showing me that you have no sense of self-control and that I can't trust you to make good judgments."

ID: "It's been two hours, and you have not gotten off your video game. Now you've blown it—no more video games for a week!"

DD: *"The video games seem to be getting in the way of your getting other things done. I need you to lay off the games for the next two days. Let's discuss this and see how we can come up with a better way to handle balancing this in a way that is reasonable."*

TT: "You are a completely spoiled brat and have no respect for me whatsoever."

ID: "How dare you speak to me that way?! Now you're not going to the mall this afternoon."

DD: *"I can't accept your talking to me in that manner. I will not take you to the mall because doing that feels like I'm supporting this poor behavior. I am asking you to please sit down with me and help me understand why you have been so angry when we talk."*

TT: "I can't depend on this kid for anything. He doesn't ever seem to care about respecting my needs."

ID: "I have had it with your coming in late! Now you're not going to the concert this Friday night."

DD: *"Look, we really need to talk. I'm not sure what's going on with your being late for your curfew. I'm really concerned about your safety, and I have some second thoughts about your going to the concert on Friday. What ideas do you have to make this work?"*

• •

I hope you feel really good about how much you have learned about the mind-set of dependable discipline and consequences so far. Now that you have learned what dependable discipline is, you can apply it when your child acts not so likable.

A Special Note About Physical Punishment

The focus of this book is parents' toxic thoughts. I believe that toxic thoughts can lead to or exacerbate physical punishment. Lowering toxic thoughts will probably reduce the likelihood of violence. If you are prone to violence with your child, however, I encourage you to seek professional help.

When I was twelve I had a friend named Allen who was a bit clumsy and heavy-handed. One day I was at his house, and Allen threw a beanbag at his sister. Unfortunately, he missed his mark and broke a window. Allen's mother screamed at him and told him that his stepfather would "discipline him" when he got home. I watched Allen literally shake with fear at the mention of his step-father. Allen's stepfather, Burt, was a burly, tough guy who was not a fan of the warm and fuzzy school of parenting. When Burt came home, I remember him asking who broke the window. Allen, to his credit, looked at his stepfather and told him that he did it. Burt sternly told Allen to go upstairs and get "the belt." When Allen re-turned, he and I sat there in the family room for the next three hours, waiting for the punishment to happen, while his stepfather nonchalantly went about his business. Burt, ruling by fear and in-timidation, thought if the consequences were postponed until later in the day, they would be more punitive. It was as if the exchange between Allen and his stepfather never took place—until Burt turned to him and said, "Let's go," and marched Allen upstairs to his room. A minute later, Allen's screams echoed through the entire house. I recall shaking inside, and probably on the outside, too.

Studies have shown that neither physical punishment, such as hit-ting and slapping, nor verbal abuse is an effective method of disci-pline. Although physical punishment may seem to give quick results, in the long term it's more harmful than helpful. Children will do what they are told to do to avoid getting spanked, but they will do what they want when no one is around to catch them. That's because they will not have learned the difference between appropriate and inappropriate behavior. In addition, physical punishment can humiliate and discourage children and can cause them to feel they are bad. Furthermore, if your child or teen is ever in serious trouble and needs your help, he will less likely reach out to you if he fears you.

The line between physical punishment and physical abuse is a fine one. I do contend that parents who mentally or physically abuse their children are likely flooded with toxic thoughts such as "You are the reason my marriage is a mess." Or "I'm going to give you a good, hard beating because it is the only way you will learn." Or "My life was great until you were born." I have, in my practice, helped many parents gain control over their toxic thoughts and attain a more level head. At the same time, this book is no substitute for professional help. For obvious reasons, I encourage parents with persistent and intense toxic thoughts to get outside counseling.

Showing children that violence is acceptable will tear down their self-esteem and can even promote physical aggression in the next generation. If you have hit your kids in the past, don't dwell in regret. We all make mistakes, and no one is perfect. However, I strongly encourage you to stop using physical punishment. Instead, apply the strategies in this book and *10 Days to a Less Defiant Child* as an alternative.

Don't Be Overly Permissive

On the other hand, being too permissive with your children can be just as problematic as being overly hard and authoritarian. Parents who are in detrimental denial, particularly, tend to be too lenient. They are inclined to think, "The world will teach my child consequences when that time comes. I really should not have to do it." Yes, the rest of the world will be happy to teach your child the consequences of his actions, and sometimes it will be painful and inconvenient for him. Only you, the parent, however, can teach him how to solve problems, make restitution, and make amends, from within the safe haven of your loving relationship.

If parents are too soft and do not respond to problematic behaviors from their child, they lose credibility and respect. I have seen defiant children with parents who are overly permissive just as often as I have seen defiant children with controlling, authoritarian parents.

Permissive parents have few consistent limits. They lack necessary rules and structure for their kids. If they do make a rule, they fail to enforce it. They put the child in charge. Permissive parents say things like "He'll go to bed when he is tired," "It's fine with me if she likes to eat ice cream for breakfast," or "She can be rude to me because I know it is just a stage."

Since children who grow up with permissive parents are used to doing whatever they want, they have trouble getting along with others. They tend to act spoiled, selfish, and, yes, quite defiant! If you are a parent who chose this laissez-faire method of parenting, don't beat yourself up about it now. You may have become overly permissive for several reasons. Maybe you grew up with strict, authoritarian parents, and consequently you decided to use very little discipline. Or maybe you chose this lenient style because you felt stressed and didn't have the energy to make rules and enforce them. Parents who are struggling with addictions to alcohol or drugs may also become compromised in the discipline department and fail to set consistent limits.

If you have erred on the overly permissive side, start to become mindful of how and where you are too permissive and make a commitment to change. Maybe you don't like conflict and have become an emotional hostage to your defiant child for fear of experiencing more drama and chaos. If this has been the case, then keep using my calm, firm, and noncontrolling approach to communicate with your child. Even if your child initially reacts negatively, keep your cool and speak with integrity. Encourage your child to dialogue with you in the same way. Point out to him that he will get more of your positive attention as well as more privileges if he can walk the calm, firm, and noncontrolling road with you. Remember that firming up your parenting style may be challenging and take some time. Your child, however, will be less defiant and respect you more in the long run.

To Sum It All Up

Keep the following points in mind as you reflect on consequences for your child:

- Having fewer toxic thoughts, being more understanding, and having a good relationship with your child are the best ways to help him learn from his mistakes and make positive changes.
- Consequences do not have to be complicated or overly emotional.
- Considering consequences carefully and using them sparingly helps all children, particularly defiant ones.
- Natural consequences will occur on their own. Collaborative logical consequences help you avoid an adversarial mentality.
- Being overly permissive is just as problematic as being overly harsh.

Chapter 9

Keeping the Positive
Energy Flowing

I HOPE YOU FEEL GOOD about how much progress you have made. By learning these powerful new skills, you're now more positive in your thoughts and emotions. Outstanding! And you are much more equipped to deal with challenging situations you face with your child. Most important, you are probably now enjoying your child more.

One couple I worked with, Rosanna and Alec, were thrilled to share how taking charge of their toxic thoughts really helped them build a more satisfying relationship with Ann Marie, their fourteen-year-old daughter, who struggled with inner anxiety and outward defiance. Rosanna shared, "Dr. Jeff, taking on a new attitude really gave us a new, easier-to-manage daughter. Until now, I never knew how much of a difference it makes to pay attention to what is going on in my own head and not let my own stuff block me from seeing what is going on with her. It is just so much easier to get along now."

All of the new skills you have gained so far have been focused on stopping and preventing your toxic thoughts. How fantastic that you now are a detoxified thinker and better skilled with consequences! You will now be far more successful in managing your child's challenging and defiant behaviors.

In this chapter, we're going to switch tacks and focus on how to keep all these positive changes going full steam ahead. Oh, sure, you will have days where you are not on top of your parenting game. But those days will be far fewer, and you'll experience PFS far less.

Putting Positive Reinforcement to Work

Although this may now seem obvious, the more positive attention you give to your child, the less he will seek attention through negative behavior. It is that simple. Kids value hearing positive support and encouragement from their parents because it feels good. Even the most defiant, brazen, and troubled kids in my office yearn for parental approval. In order to meet your child's needs for positive attention, you need to be in the right mind-set.

Positive reinforcement generates a lot of positive energy. Rewards and positive responses encourage your child to continue positive behaviors or engage in new ones. Although this may seem easy to do, too many parents get negative results by using it improperly. And then the power of positive reinforcement goes out the window.

Rewards Work Because They Feel Good

The appeal of using rewards with children is that they are great motivators. If you think about it, any time you really desire to do something, it's because it will be pleasurable for you. When your child gets a smile, compliment, or hug from you, he feels good. Rewards are a powerful tool that can further encourage your child to behave better, or more cooperatively, almost instantly.

Children who tend to be more defiant especially need to be rewarded when they make good choices. They need the extra positive incentive to compensate for their negative feelings about themselves.

Positive Reinforcement Creates More Positive Changes

I am discussing positive reinforcement near the end of this book for a reason. Before you successfully detoxified, it probably was quite difficult for you to find opportunities to reward your challenging-to-like child. But now that you think less toxically, I bet that you're seeing a better relationship with your child and fewer defiant behaviors. You are now in a new and better position where you can "catch" your child's positive behaviors. When you "catch" and reward your child's positive behaviors, you increase the chance he will continue to act that way. The more that you encourage positive behavior in your child, the more problem behavior is discouraged. This is true because:

- Your child can't be both cooperative and difficult at the same time. The more compliance, the less defiance.
- The more you focus on your child's emerging positive actions and behaviors that show increased compliance, the more you will see these encouraging changes.

Staying Mindful of Staying Positive

I have discussed the importance of being mindful to tune in to and overcome your toxic thoughts. It is also critical that you be mindful of being positive with your child. The big reason that many parents do not provide their children enough positive feedback is that they don't keep it as a parenting priority. In the same way that catching your toxic thoughts becomes a healthy habit, so does seeking to give your child positive reinforcement.

If you recall, in Chapter 4, I stressed the importance of being grateful for all that you have in life and for your child's health and positive qualities. Unfortunately, parents tend to take their children's positive qualities and behaviors for granted. "It took Guiana months to *finally* clean up her room, so why should I notice, or even say 'Thank you' when she does her chores?" asked Nancy, a frustrated mom.

Remember to catch your child doing appropriate behaviors. The more you catch those positive behaviors, the more you can store them up to use as evidence for alternatives to detoxify your toxic thoughts. See that? You have now come full circle: Detoxifying your thoughts helps free you up to find positive behaviors in your child and staying mindful of the positives helps you to detoxify. This is why positive reinforcement gives you more ways to nail the toxic-thought coffin shut.

The Positive-Reinforcement Habit Is Not Easy

Yes, I get it. Parenting is challenging. You have a bird's-eye view of your child's negative behaviors—the refusal to cooperate, the refusal to do homework, the refusal to tell the truth about why she was not home on time. I'll grant you that it is not always easy to look for the positives. Before you detoxified, you may even have learned to *expect* negative behaviors.

Don't feel too bad about overlooking the positives with your child. I also see, in relationships between employee and employer, husband and wife, and brother and sister—even in friendships— that people neglect to focus on the positive. Think about it: When your boss calls you into the office, your first thought isn't "I'm going to be praised." It's usually "Uh-oh! What did I do wrong?"

The problem is that kids typically get (or think they are getting) more attention for negative behaviors. So they pick senseless arguments with you, slam doors, quarrel with siblings, and do anything else they can think of that will push your toxic-thinking button. In a very extreme example, a seventeen-year-old girl made a suicide attempt to get her parents' attention. Fortunately, after working with me, she and her parents began to understand each other more and became much closer. Yet she continued to assert that her attempt on her life was the only way to get her concerns taken seriously.

Perhaps your child actually does not consciously realize that when he misbehaves, he gets a lot of your attention. But guess what? He knows it nonetheless. Kids may not always be rational, but they are very good at finding ways to get what they want most— your attention.

Parents struggle with the idea that their focus on bad behavior only encourages it, because it seems so illogical. One mother I worked with really struggled with this: "Why would Chantal *want* to be yelled at? Why would it be preferable to walking in from school and saying hello, even to being ignored?"

Your child goes for the negative attention because he will get a powerful and often quick response from you. Adding to his motivation is that he knows you may feel bad and even possibly apologize to him, which he will perceive as feeling good. Certainly, the more you detoxify your thoughts, the less this will happen. Realize, however, that even if you have detoxified to the max, your child, by definition, is still maturing. So when your child continues to misbehave, keep his maturity deficits in mind, before your resentment keeps you from seeing positive behaviors.

Children can be impulsive and blurt out comments that can be hurtful. I am all for calling your child on misbehavior or disrespect. At the same time, if you can separate the wheat from the chaff and focus more on the positive behaviors, you and your child will be better off. As you lessen your emotional reactivity, the more you will bypass your child's overreactivity. Thinking less toxically is a huge step in that direction.

But I Shouldn't Have to Bribe My Kid

Many parents seem to resent giving positive attention and rewards when their child still behaves badly. They think, "I shouldn't have to bribe her to act the right way." Ouch, here goes that "should" (in this case "shouldn't") thinking again. Well-meaning parents can confuse rewards with bribes.

Many parents also insist that rewards don't work to encourage their children to behave well. I ask these parents if they are using rewards to stop an inappropriate behavior rather than to encourage appropriate behavior. When one of my daughters was in preschool, I remember a parent trying to coax her crying and clinging child to calm down by saying, "If you stop crying, I will take you out for ice cream later." Now that's a bribe, not positive reinforcement. Though I really do understand why parents do this—no one wants to be the parent of an out-of-control child in public, as it's uncomfortable and embarrassing—using a reward this way really is a form of bribery, and it often does no work.

Hang in there—it does get confusing in the heat of battle. The problem with this way of giving reinforcement is that your child realizes that by crying at school, he can get ice cream when he stops. The *negative* behavior has been rewarded. Your teen will quickly realize that if he *keeps* his room a mess, eventually he'll be offered a reward, whether it is going to the mall or playing a video game, for cleaning it up.

Because positive reinforcement is associated with rewards—both verbal and nonverbal—parents also sometimes confuse "rewarding" with "spoiling." Jules, father of twelve-year-old Barry, recently commented to me, "You know, Barry still gives me crap with his attitude. Now you are telling me to stroke this kid and have me make a big deal for what he should be doing normally anyway. Seems to me he'll get more spoiled or expect me to give him rewards all the time!"

This is a great point and one I hear quite a bit. I asked Jules to think about himself for a moment (something frustrated parents need to be reminded to do).

Jeff: "I see you have a golf shirt on. Do you like to play golf?"

Jules: "Yeah, it's the one thing that keeps me sane. I try to play one time a week, at least."

Jeff: "So you do your daily grind, and golf is kind of like a reward and it keeps your stress level down?"

Jules: "Yeah, I guess so. What's your point?"

Jeff: "And you still play golf even if you lose it at home or have a rough few days at work?"

Jules: "Well, of course, golf keeps me feeling good even when things aren't always so wonderful."

Jeff: "So you could say that playing golf even if you aren't always hitting winning parenting shots with Barry is still a good thing for you to do."

Jules: "Absolutely. It's worth the effort."

Jeff: "Jules, it seems like golf is your reward for your effort at work and as a dad. Yet it is a certainly not a bribe for you to try to do well in these areas of your life."

Jules: "Okay, well, if you put it that way, I see what you're saying. My golf is my way of helping me feel good. Yes, I guess it is positive reinforcement, even though I am far from perfect. I guess it is unfair to wait till Barry outgrows his grouchiness before I make more effort to see his positive exceptions and do nice things for him."

Jules got my point exactly. In the world of work, most people go to their job every day, show up on time, work hard, and are rewarded, not bribed or spoiled, by a paycheck. They deserve it for all their hard work. And wherever you are, if you are kind to others, you are usually rewarded when their kindness is offered back to you. The common theme here is that all of these "rewards" feel good and increase the chance that you will continue to choose these positive behaviors. These are examples of positive reinforcement in action.

As I'll soon discuss, rewards don't always have to be, nor is it best they always be, material. In fact, the most powerful kind of reward a parent has to offer is simple, doesn't cost anything, and is always at hand—it's verbal praise. This is when a parent says, "I am so proud of you for this morning. You didn't cry and cling to Mommy. You went right into school. You are such a brave girl." Or as another example, the parent who remarks, "I really appreciate how you ignored your sister when she provoked you." Or finally, the parent of a teen who says, "Hey, I gotta give it you for cleaning up your room as I asked before you go out. Thanks for getting it done so promptly."

Make Sure Your Expectations Are Not Too High

Some parents refrain from rewarding their kids because their expectations of them are too high. Let me say loud and clear that it is imperative for parents to encourage their children to strive toward reasonably challenging goals. At the same time, if parents have rigid expectations that are over the top, then children can feel set up to fail. This could then have the opposite effect, that is, demotivation.

The first time I met with seventeen-year-old Rafael, it was immediately clear that he felt disempowered by his parents' unrealistic expectations. Rafael had worked the previous summer as a doorman at a Philadelphia hotel and also as a waiter in a popular restaurant. He had managed to save up more than $6,000, but his parents had wanted him to earn $7,500 during the summer to help pay for college. Rafael's father, Luis, was a highly successful financial planner, and his mother, Roberta, was an emergency room physician. Although I am no accountant, it seemed clear that this family was not destined for financial hardship anytime soon.

Luis and Roberta both had complained to me that Rafael was not applying himself enough, and that is why he did not earn the extra $1,500. When we had time alone, Rafael shared that the previous year his older sister had received a full scholarship to an Ivy League college. Rafael, hardworking but not an academic superstar, felt that nothing he did was good enough.

Rafael was initially reluctant to tell his parents how he felt. During this session, when I asked both parents if they were proud of Rafael, they said, "Of course." Rafael said he didn't believe them, and told them how he felt. Both parents began to cry and realized they had been playing a significant role in Rafael's despair. Luis and Roberta began to see how their son struggled to keep up with the family's intensity and achievements.

From that moment on, Luis and Roberta adjusted their expectations to a more realistic level. Rafael was astonished when his mother and father told him they were proud of him for getting a C+ on a very difficult chemistry test. Chemistry had been Rafael's most difficult subject. Hearing praise for what used to be a huge point of contention left him feeling relieved and inspired him to be more motivated.

Verbal Praise Has Maximum Impact

Verbal praise is the best kind of reward because it doesn't come from a store or cost anything. And most important, it's more meaningful to your child than getting a toy or treat. As you saw above, it meant the world to Rafael.

Of course, giving other kinds of rewards, like more video game time, a new toy, or candy, to cooperative kids is not necessarily inappropriate or wrong. In some situations, it can be an appropriate and effective way to further encourage positive behavior. (See below for more advice on giving material rewards.)

That said, I have never met a child or an adult who did not deep down want her parents to say, "We're so proud of you." Or "I really admire the time and hard work you put into that." People of all ages crave the approval of their parents.

You, as the parent, are a powerful person to your child. You always have been, and you always will be. Sincere praise from you has mega-emotional weight. And whether your child is nine months, nine years, or twenty-nine years old, he always wants to know that you're proud of him.

How to Verbally Praise Your Child

When you do praise your child, it's important to make sure your praise is meaningful. When giving praise, it's critical to keep the following points in mind:

1. Just do it. As much as I am a huge advocate of praising children, there have been times, with my own kids, when I was too concerned about whether it was the right time or right thing to do. My advice, in this case, is to stop thinking and to start sharing. Some parents fear that if they praise too much, their child will rebel against the praise. As long as you are not going overboard with compliments twenty-four hours a day, seven days a week, I don't think you can praise your child enough for the positive moves she makes. (See Table 9.1 for some suggestions on when to praise.)

2. Be real. Even though defiant children in particular view themselves as your equal, they also hold feelings of shame. Some children that I work with have a hard time believing their parents' praise because they view it as insincere. The great news is that to be sincere, all you need to do is speak from your heart. I recently heard one father tell his fourteen-year-old daughter, "I'm proud of you for telling me about your friend pressuring you to smoke." Once she saw her father truly meant this, she believed his compliment was meaningful.

3. Be specific. Your praise also will be perceived as more sincere and powerful when you make it specific. Telling your child what you are specifically praising him for makes your comment more believable, and it helps him know exactly what he is doing so well. Comments such as "Thanks for saying please and thank you" help your child know exactly what they did that you appreciate. This is more effective than saying "You had good manners today." Saying "I really liked how you helped me load and unload the groceries with no complaints" is more specific than "I liked your behavior after we went shopping."

So remember that it's important that you let your child know exactly what he did that was different from before and why it was helpful. Here are a couple more examples:

"Thanks for clearing up the food crumbs off the table without me asking you to. This really helped me focus on getting the kitchen counters cleaned up while you did that." "I really appreciated how you accepted, without carrying on, that I could not give your friend a ride to her job."

4. Less is more. Many well-meaning parents talk too much. I have certainly made this mistake many times. To avoid your child thinking that you are being insincere, make your positive comment and then zip it—stop talking about it. Keep it simple: "You were so patient and helpful in the store today." If she shrugs it off, like she doesn't care, don't be fooled. You don't have to convince her by saying, "Oh, no, really! I couldn't get over how much better you were . . . " She heard your praise, and it made her feel good. Trust in the power of your positive words and let it go.

5. The sooner the better. Try to deliver praise as soon as possible after spotting the appropriate behavior or the right decision. The longer the delay, the smaller the impact will be and the less likely it will motivate more desirable behavior. Naturally, a few

Table 9.1   Sample behaviors to praise and reward

Making a new friend	Offering to help	Being flexible	Resolving conflict
Making bed	Not interrupting	Not interrupting	Using humor
Sharing toys	Using good manners	Starting homework	Finishing homework
Asking for help	Speaking quietly	Walking softly	Apologizing
Cleaning room	Walking dog	Taking out trash	Being friendly
Being honest	Waking up on time	Showering	Brushing teeth
Being patient	Being open	Speaking softly	Being calm or relaxed

praiseworthy moments might pass you by, especially in the beginning. It's still okay to bring it up by saying, "I meant to tell you: I noticed how you shared your toys with your brother today. That was very considerate of you."

6. Be random and varied. Avoid saying the same thing every time you praise your child. The more your verbal reward varies, the more captivating it will be. Dr. B. F. Skinner taught us this. Catch your child starting his homework early or studying some afternoon. Moving beyond just verbal praise, spontaneously giving him a new music CD or that long-awaited new snowboard will also have a big impact on his motivation. Think about this for a minute: When someone passes you every day and says "hi" with the same tone and demeanor, you may start to get distracted and gradually stop noticing. If, however, the person you pass acts more animated or asks you questions, you may become more tuned in. If you say "Great job" every time your child does something good, that compliment will start to lose meaning. She'll think you're on autopilot, and she'll be right. Varying your comments will help your child continue to perceive your praise as honest and heartfelt.

Finding Praiseworthy Behaviors

Table 9.1 lists positive behaviors that deserve praise. Feel free to photocopy it and place it somewhere for easy reference. It will serve as a helpful reminder for you to identify and reward your child's positive behaviors. Blank lines are provided at the bottom so that you can include any behaviors specific to your child.

Spicing It Up with Other Rewards

Though I think praise is the best reward a parent can give on a daily basis, there are times when other rewards can work in conjunction with praise to further encourage positive behavior in your child. A new action figure, bottle of nail polish, video game, or item of clothing keeps things interesting and unpredictable.

I mentioned the famous psychologist B. F. Skinner above. His theories about positive reinforcement are quite complex, but there are two major conclusions he reached that are very important to your situation. First, Dr. Skinner showed that behaviors are controlled by rewards. Second, he taught us that when we don't know what the rewards are, or when they will occur, we get even more motivated. This is why kids like surprise boxes and many adults like gambling casinos.

Follow these five steps when giving nonverbal rewards to your child:

1. Remember to involve your child. The most powerful rewards are those genuinely desired. Ask your child to sit down with you and review the lists in tables 9.2 or 9.3. Come up with a few options together and agree to use them. This gives your child a goal to work toward.

2. Don't use nonverbal rewards to replace verbal ones. Use other kinds of rewards as a complement to your verbal praising

Table 9.2   Reward possibilities for preschool/elementary age

Playing with clay or Playdough	Going someplace alone with Mom or Dad	Helping plan the day's activities
Helping Mom or Dad	Having a longer time in the bathtub	Riding on a bicycle with Dad or Mom
Going out for ice cream	Playing with friends	Feeding a pet
Going to the park	Playing in the sandbox	Making noises with rattles, pans, or bells
Playing a board game with Dad or Mom	Going to the library	Drawing with crayons
Bouncing on the bed	Playing outside	Time to play a computer game or visit a fun Web site
Staying up late	Going on a trip to the zoo	Renting a video game
Reading a book together	Riding on Dad's shoulders	Eating out

when you feel your child has shown a strong, positive change or accomplishment, such as making the honor roll at school, getting a B (or even a C+) on a difficult test, or not arguing with his brother for two weeks. Many younger children find candy rewarding. Table 9.2 suggests rewards for preschool- and elementary-age children, table 9.3 for teenagers.

3. Tune in to what your child values and to what is healthy and actually valuable to them. It's easy to give kids candy or ice cream as a reward, but this can lead to too much sugar and even encourage obesity in some kids. It's helpful to know what your child values besides sugary treats and use them instead or as well. Extra TV time, phone privileges, a sleepover with friends, a Saturday at the mall—most kids enjoy these things and will perceive them as powerful incentives.

4. Reward after good behavior. To avoid the bribery scenario, give your child a reward only after she has behaved in an appropriate or desirable way.

Table 9.3   Reward possibilities for preteens/teens

Talking additional time on the telephone	Hanging out with a friend	Making a trip alone that is deemed safe
Finding a part-time job	Taking the car to school for a day	Getting to stay out later than usual
Receiving money for a new purchase	Getting a surprise	Going to an amusement park
Going shopping with friends	Inviting a friend to eat out	Getting to sleep in late on the weekend
Having their own checking account	Receiving a magazine subscription	Being allowed to sit alone with a friend when the family eats out
Going to a movie theater with a friend	Playing a video game	Renting a new video game
Watching a video	Haircut or hairstyle	Skateboarding
Redecorating their own room	Participating in activities with friends	Going to summer camp

5. *Don't forget to follow through.* Many parents worry too much about following through on punishments instead of following through on rewards. If you say you are going to give your child a reward, make sure you do it. You'd be surprised how many parents I have seen renege on their agreements with their kids and then freak out when those same kids later don't do what they had promised.

Take a look at the tables for ideas to reward both younger and older children. Keep in mind that these groupings are not meant to be exhaustive; rather, they are ideas to get you started.

Encourage the Effort, for It Counts a Lot, Too

Though we've talked a great deal about behavior and accomplishments, your child's efforts are just as important. I have talked with many adults who still struggle with the lack of encouragement they received during their childhoods. Praise and other rewards are powerful tools, but I also want to stress encouragement. Encouragement focuses on your child's efforts. Praise focuses on results. Both are valuable in reinforcing appropriate behaviors. To help give solid encouragement to your child, try the following:

1. *Be accepting.* As in the earlier example with Rafael, parents who are high achievers sometimes unwittingly (or wittingly) send the message that they accept their child as long as he performs to his parents' standards. Because all children have a fundamental need to belong, to feel accepted and wanted—especially by their parents—making your acceptance conditional on achievements can undermine your child's self-esteem.

2. *Bestow confidence.* All children can learn, even though some may take longer than others to master a concept or a skill. Your confidence in your child's ability to keep going when she feels frustrated and defeated, your confidence that he'll eventually succeed, your confidence that he'll make something useful of his life—this is the encouragement that can make the difference between success and failure. To show confidence, you really have to believe that your child is realistically capable of success. If you don't believe in her, then she has to overcome your doubts as well as her own.

3. *Look for past examples of achievements to encourage your child to take the next step.* We all do well by recalling our past successes. Anchoring yourself in past successes can provide motivation in new challenges. Difficult children tend to dismiss what they did well in the past. You can encourage your child by reminding him in a calm, firm, and noncontrolling way of what he has done well in the past. This is demonstrated in the following example: "You did a great job working hard in math last year, especially when you wanted to give up because it was so challenging. I know you feel like giving up right now, but you have shown the ability to get through difficult subjects before."

4. Break larger tasks into smaller ones. Breaking challenges down is so effective because it helps kids slow down their thoughts and emotions and prevents them from overreacting. Challenging children lack flexibility and can easily become overwhelmed. Here is an example of how words of encouragement can be used to reduce the stress that comes with difficult challenges: "I know this report is a little longer, but I'll bet if you break it down into sections, it will come out really well when you are done."

Keeping the Like Flowing

Following the title of this book, it is important that we remind our kids that we not only love them but also like them. It's important to do your best to let your child know through your words and actions that you love, like, and value her. Now that you have gained considerable skills in reducing your toxic thinking, try to keep the message of how you like who your child is as free and unconditional as possible. Statements such as these will be deeply appreciated by your child:

- "I really like how you make me laugh."
- "I like the time we share when we go shopping together."
- "I know you're disappointed about not making the team, but I like how you tried your best, and that's what's important."
- "I like how cool it is that you are now so into music."

Here are some further suggestions for creating an encouraging and supportive atmosphere for your child:

- Be liberal in showing your understanding and love.
- Try to be patient and understanding about her mistakes and any temporary setbacks.
- Don't criticize her in front of others.

- Take time daily to listen and talk to your child and show interest in her activities.
- Don't be afraid to touch, hug, and kiss your child.
- Let her know that no matter what happens, you will always love her.

Keeping Your Tank Full, Too

The focus of this book so far has been on skills that you can use to promote your child's self-esteem and overall emotional health. Think of the thought and energy you are putting into your parenting! You are willing to try to improve yourself as a parent, and that is something I hope you are very proud of. By giving yourself credit, you are also helping your child. The better you feel about yourself, the better your child will feel about herself. See "Giving Yourself Credit as a Parent" to make sure you reinforce your own efforts, too.

Giving Yourself Credit as a Parent

Go through the list of positive behaviors below and pat yourself on the back for all the ones you can check off:

Helped with potty training	_____
Attended a game	_____
Cooked meals	_____
Enrolled child in a sport	_____
Exposed child to a religious faith	_____
Picked out clothes	_____
Gave baths	_____
Taught to tie shoes	_____
Helped teach to read	_____

Helped with homework   ____
Took to playdates   ____
Read stories at night   ____
Attended teacher conferences   ____
Took bowling   ____
Hosted sleepovers   ____
Provided affection   ____
Attended school concerts   ____
Watched sports events   ____
Expressed love   ____
Decorated house for holidays   ____
Listened to briefings of the day   ____
Loved despite defiance directed at you   ____

No matter how many of the above positive parenting behaviors you have done, I am encouraging you to feel good about those you checked off. As you will see in the next section, how you talk to yourself plays a big role in how you feel about all the great things you have done and the mistakes you have made.

● ●

Positive Self-Talk with the Parent in the Mirror

I first introduced the concept of self-talk in Chapter 2. My point then was to help you realize how much we all talk to ourselves. I have coached you to overcome toxic thoughts about your kids. Remember, the way you think drives how you will feel and act.

Negative self-talk such as "I never should have been a parent" or "I'm hopeless" will reduce your confidence. Pay closer attention to your self-talk and do your best to keep it positive. When your self-talk is positive, you are likely to be calmer and more relaxed. For example, if you say to yourself, "I feel good about how I handled that conflict" or "I'm glad I did not yell," you are praising yourself and you will feel less stressed.

You will feel much better about your parenting efforts if you stay mindful of all the positive things you have done for your child. I also encourage you to be wary of any negative self-talk messages you may give yourself such as:

- "I'm a mean dad."
- "I'm an impatient mother."
- "I never get a moment to myself."
- "Everyone takes, takes, takes, and no one gives to me."

As I said earlier on, parents have a lot of shame when they think about and treat their kids negatively. Stay vigilant for the distorted thoughts that signal that you are being irrationally hard on yourself. These thoughts will do nothing other than leave you feeling beaten down and drained. Using the same model of disputing toxic thoughts about your kids, challenge those you hold about yourself. Examples of counterthoughts are presented here:

"I'm a lousy parent." (Actually, I am a caring parent who just became overwhelmed.)

"I should know better." (I will do myself a favor by remembering not to "should" all over myself.)

"No other parents struggle like me." (It is pretty clear that this book was not just written for me.)

"It is never going to get easier." (I will feel better when I reflect on the times that are easier.)

"My child does not behave as well as others." (This may not be true, and even if it is, the good news is that I am doing all I can to help my child be less distressed.)

As you may recall from when I discussed "label gluing," if you give your child a negative label, he will live up to it. The same applies to you. Trashing yourself as a parent makes matters only worse and diminishes all your previous efforts and the changes you have made. This kind of negative thinking leads to withdrawal and influences parents to throw their hands in the air and give up. This "Why bother trying anymore?" attitude was once poignantly described by a parent as "Why rearrange the furniture on the *Titanic*?" as he shared the feeling that he could never overcome the conflicts he had with his very defiant daughter. Fortunately, his ship did not sink because he and his daughter worked through their problems even though there were still occasional rough waters.

If you make it a point to avoid these negative thoughts about yourself and your parenting situation, you will feel better. Following is a list of alternatives to any negative self-talk. I encourage you to pick the ones that resonate with who you are as a parent. Then do yourself a favor and stand in the mirror and say them to yourself. Speak loud and proud. I know this may seem corny, but I think you will be moved by doing this. Most of the time when we look in the mirror it is to fix our hair or make sure our clothes match. I am encouraging you to look closer, and deeper. As you say any of the following, remember that you are doing this to like the parent you love—you. Here is a sampling of alternatives to those negative messages:

- "I feel good about being calm, firm, and noncontrolling in stating boundaries, even if they aren't immediately accepted."
- "Even though I made a mistake, I can still try to be the best mom I can be."
- "I can take some time for myself and not feel guilty."
- "I am a good parent."
- "I may make mistakes, but that does not make me a less valuable person."
- "This is an opportunity to teach my child something new."

- "I just need to take one step at a time and do what I can."
- "Being calm, firm, and noncontrolling helps me stay centered and less reactive."
- "Just because I slipped and yelled today does not mean I have to keep doing it."
- "I can pick my battles wisely to gain my child's cooperation."
- "I am not helpless. I have people and resources to call upon if I need to."
- "In the big picture, this is really not a big deal."

Give Yourself Other Rewards

Don't forget to reward yourself once in a while in material ways as well. After all, being a parent is challenging. Think about it this way: By giving to yourself, you are giving a better self to your child. Some examples of rewards you might enjoy include:

- Getting your nails done ·
- Taking a soothing bath
- Buying a new book or magazine
- Going out for dinner
- Getting away overnight or for a weekend without children
- Exercising
- Staying connected to your spirituality
- Taking a new adult education class
- Buying a new outfit
- Reading a new book you've been interested in
- Taking up gardening
- Doing fun things with your friends
- Keeping your marriage nourished
- Trying rock climbing
- Playing pool
- Bowling

- Playing cards
- Taking up quilting
- Bike riding
- Occasional long walks around the neighborhood or hiking
- Joining a local gym
- Participating in a yoga class
- Taking day trips to historic sites or museums
- Attending a lecture in a topic you are interested in

To Sum It All Up

Today you have learned about the power of praise and other rewards to reinforce positive behaviors in your child. Keep in mind the following key points:

- Praise, if given in the correct manner, can significantly increase your child's positive behaviors.
- Increasing positive behaviors lowers defiant behaviors.
- Rewards can be combined with praise to recognize your child's positive behaviors.
- Encouraging your child's efforts and freely expressing like, as well as love, are very important.
- Reinforcing yourself for your positive parenting efforts and actions is very valuable to both you and your child.

Chapter 10

Liking the Child You Love over the Long Run

CONGRATULATIONS on completing this program! Now that you have learned to overcome your toxic thoughts, no longer will you be plagued by Parent Frustration Syndrome. Detoxifying your thinking will keep changing your parenting life for the better. Yes, it takes work, but taking responsibility for your own parenting thoughts, actions, and feelings is important. In the words of famous author, psychiatrist, and concentration camp survivor Viktor Frankl, "The last of human freedoms is the ability to choose one's attitude in a given set of circumstances."

You have come so far in liking the child you love. I hope you're feeling good about your progress. As you reflect on all that you have achieved to improve your relationship with your child, let's take a quick look at the highlights of what you have accomplished so far. You have:

- Discovered the nine toxic thoughts of parenting and how they cause your PFS
- Learned valuable relaxation and self-comfort skills to prepare you to detoxify your parenting mind
- Gained mindful awareness of your toxic thoughts as they occur

- Discovered how to create and use alternatives to eliminate your toxic thoughts
- Learned the power of collaborative logical consequences
- Become skilled in using positive reinforcement to encourage continued positive changes in your child and in yourself

As I was in the process of writing this last chapter, I was in a local mall and heard a loud "Hey, it's Dr. Jeff!" from Josh, a fifteen-year-old boy whom I had worked with along with his family. As I approached Josh and his mom, Josh hugged her and said, "Hey, you never thought I'd be like this with my mom in public, did you?" I laughed and said, "Josh, there was a time when your parents were scared to take you out in public!" We all laughed and reminisced about the wonderful changes Josh's parents made that paved the way for him to follow suit.

I am pleased to say that these strategies also transformed my own life as a parent. As I learned to change my own perspective and parenting behaviors, my relationship with my kids also changed for the better. I am by no means a perfect parent and still have work to do, yet I am grateful for having made these changes in my life.

We all have to keep working at our parenting skills. In Chapter 5, I mentioned how being mindful is like bathing—it is best done on an ongoing basis. The same goes for everything else you have learned in this book. I guarantee that if you truly embrace these strategies, your parent-child relationship will become more emotionally healthy than you ever could have imagined.

Embrace the Continuous Challenge

Staying free of toxic thinking takes ongoing discipline and work. The reality, however, is that the more you detoxify, the easier it becomes. Yes, there still will be trying times when you may not be at the top of your parenting game. Also be aware that as you detoxify, your child may actually try to test you even more with provo- cations. Why? Because your child was conditioned by your unhealthy thoughts, emotions, and behaviors. You have now become a much more emotionally centered parent, and your child notices this. She may actually have a hard time accepting that you are no longer a toxic-thinking parent, or at least much less of one. She naturally may want to "road test" you to see if you are really going to relate to her in an emotionally smarter manner. Stay positive yet realistic in your expectations, and please don't give up when your child puts the pedal to the metal. If you continue to practice what you've learned so far and push forward, you and your child will be moving in the right direction.

Treasure Your Setbacks

Remember, you are not going for perfection. Realize that setbacks are inevitable, and they never seem minor in the moment. Don't get too down on yourself if and when you go toxic in the future. In the words of Rocky Balboa, "It ain't about how hard you can hit, it's about how hard you can get hit and keep moving forward." I am talking about having a resilient spirit as a parent. To this day, I still have to work at overcoming my own toxic thoughts. When I find myself getting mired in them, I give myself a pat on the back for being tuned in and working through them. I hope you will do the same.

Parents don't wake up and plan to have toxic thoughts toward their kids. No, the toxic train wreck often results from other stressors popping up faster than you can handle. You may have a harder time resisting toxic thoughts when the juice gets knocked over on the table or the grocery bag breaks as it lands short of the counter and everything in it spills onto the floor. Keep this also in mind when the dog has an accident on the rug. Try to remember to see these transient crises as opportunities to keep your cool versus acting like a raving fool.

Speaking of a past crisis that catalyzed me into toxic thoughts, I recall taking my children camping years ago. I was so pumped up to give my kids a wonderful memory while we braved the great outdoors. Of course, I was trying to deny the "sprinkle" as we drove to the campground. Unfortunately, this gentle rain became a torrential downpour just when we got the tent up. No worries, right? After all, we were secure in the tent.

The calm lasted very briefly. One of my young children saw a scary spider inside the tent. Amid all three screaming, my oldest tried to escape the tent and got her hair caught in the zipper. My youngest, still in pull-ups, had an untimely, to say the least, "accident." All this happened within the span of less than a minute. While I was in the far reaches of the country, I suddenly found myself in Toxic-Thought City. I noted how crazy the situation must have looked to neighboring campers. The tent was bobbing up and down with my daughter's hair caught in it while all of us were trying to get out. To this day we laugh at this memory, but at the time it was not one of those magical moments.

Most satisfying for me was that in that situation I kept my cool and didn't freak out. Detoxifying my thoughts in real time was not easy. Keeping my cool during our camping trip by no means meant that I was always "Mr. Calm" from that day forward. But it did give me a solid foothold to keep striving to be a more patient father.

Another time, I did not have as much grace. One of my children accidentally threw a ball that landed on a tray of red paint on an art table in my home. I had not witnessed this, but as I returned home, my young son courageously came up to me and apprised me of what had happened. I literally saw red as I learned that red paint had splattered all over a freshly and professionally painted white wall. My kids will never forget how much their dad cursed in that ten-minute span. I was not justified in carrying on so. At the same time, having just put up my townhouse for sale with a showing scheduled thirty minutes after discovering the unexpected splatter art, I had developed serious, acute PFS. Yes, I had a few toxic thoughts that day.

I realized later that my freaking out did not portray me as the kind of role model I aspire to be. Fortunately, it was another lesson learned, and I continued to work on controlling my toxic thoughts and my temper. I also encourage you to learn from any setbacks, put them behind you, and keep moving forward.

Be a "Team Parent"

In corporate America, organizational life, and sports, being a team player is highly valued. Team players are those who keep their own needs and egos from usurping the greater good of the organization. In contrast, those who complain and seek to undermine others are not team players, and they can do a lot of damage.

You and your child are a team. Keeping your toxic thoughts from dividing the two of you goes a long way in helping you stay emotionally connected. Homework issues, sibling quarrels, school problems, peer conflicts, and chore issues can easily lead parents and children to become adversarial, unless you keep in mind that you are in it together.

Your kids very much want your approval. Beyond the material possessions you provide, your child depends on you for validation and acceptance. Even when she does not act like it, she needs your like, love, and understanding. She wants you to be on her team and also a huge fan.

As a parent who is now knowledgeable about toxic thoughts, you know how ignoring problems only makes them fester. Being a team parent means being willing to talk out disagreements and differences. The more you try to understand where your child is coming from, the more she will feel that you are standing right beside her. Your best effort is in trying to join with, rather than work against, your child's will.

Stay Accountable

At different points in this book I have pointed out the value of writing down thoughts and feelings. One parent I worked with thought it would make him a "pathetic soul." He said, "Dr. Jeff, the last thing I want to do is dwell on what is bothering me about my kids by writing down the problems." It was not until he punched a hole in a wall in anger that he was willing to deal with his toxic thoughts and PFS more constructively. This client needed a way to stay more emotionally accountable. The more you stay accountable to your thoughts and feelings as a parent, the easier, and more effective, your parenting will be.

Writing down your thoughts and feelings actually makes you much more of a doer than a dweller. Interestingly, this same father had tried to lose weight several times in his life, and he was not successful until he kept track of his daily calories by writing them down. He realized that keeping on top of unhealthy thoughts was just as helpful as keeping track of unhealthy food.

In the box appendix on page 226, I have included a worksheet that you can either copy or adapt in your own journal. As you can see, there is a column for the triggering event, the resulting toxic thought, and the alternative you can use to dispute the thought. Whether you use any of the formats I have provided in this book or another format of your choice, progress occurs when you start recording your toxic thoughts and more rational alternatives to them. I recommend that you also record the positive changes you see in yourself and in your child. The log does not have to be formal or elaborate. Any format that keeps track of your thoughts and feelings and your positive breakthroughs and successes will be helpful.

Remember to give yourself and your child time to get used to your new approach. Sticking to the changes you make is key. You must keep in mind that this is a work in progress, and keep using these strategies for the long haul.

Humbly Spread the Word

I hope you are very excited now that you have learned how much you can control your thoughts and feelings. The truth, however, is that not everyone will be willing to do the work you have done. Some parents you come into contact with may opt to solely focus on their children's challenging behaviors. They may reject the idea that their toxic thoughts play a big role in their children's problem behaviors and their relationships with their kids.

I certainly don't recommend that you run up to all the stressed-out parents you see and try to show them the light. If you tell them that they, and not their children, are the ones who are in charge of how they think and feel, they may not warmly receive your message. What you can keep in mind, however, is that you and I, and thousands of other readers, know that this is pretty much the truth.

There are certainly enough people out there who offer unwelcome advice. However, I encourage you to share these ideas with those who are receptive to them. The more that you help other willing parents see how their toxic thoughts cause their PFS, the more this will reinforce and strengthen your own thought-detoxifying knowledge and skills. Remember that we teach best what we need to learn.

If you are interested, feel free to visit my Web site, www.Dr Jeffonline.com, and sign up for my quarterly complimentary e-mail newsletter. I will continue to provide updates on my work in helping free parents like you from toxic thoughts. I have also included references of other books on the topic of cognitive therapy in the "Recommended Reading" section of this book.

Remember to Have Fun

It is important to remind ourselves to enjoy our time with our children as much as possible. The sobering reality is that life can deliver the unexpected and be much shorter than we could ever imagine.

As I said earlier, we all have many blessings to count. In Chapter 4 I talked about having fun on getaways and vacations. Don't forget to have fun in daily life as well. Make each day count with your children. The little fun moments in life become treasured memories. Going swimming and safely throwing each other around a pool can be a blast. Watching funny movies together can lead to great laughs. Taking your teen out for a walk can be fun and relaxing.

The more you tune in to joy, the more you can remind yourself to find it in yourself and your family. Better yet, infuse your life with joy and good times and be a role model to remind other parents and children to follow your positive lead.

Some Final Words

Loving children comes easy to most parents. Liking them when they are challenging, difficult, or defiant is not so easy. Remember that when children are most unlovable, that is when you must love them the most. And when children are most unlikable, this is when you must learn to like them the most. It takes courage to open yourself up to finding new ways to understand and relate to your child, especially when you are frustrated with him. I commend you on the effort you have put forth in reading this book and tuning in to your thoughts

Remember that progress, not perfection, is what you are striving for. Children can be very challenging and can also be very rewarding. You have learned many wonderful new ideas and strategies. I wish you happiness and joy in using them.

The next time you look at your child and tell him how much you love him, let him also know how much you like him. Liking the child you love will open up new windows of understanding and connection with your child. And you will like yourself more than ever for doing this.

Acknowledgments

Thanks to all of my clients over the past twenty years. I am honored that so many parents and kids along the way have shared their pain, losses, struggles, and triumphs with me. You have all taught me so much about how to be a psychologist and about how much more I need to keep learning.

Mom and Dad, thanks for being wonderful parents. You have always shown that you loved me, even during the rare times you didn't like me. How masterful you have been in still helping me believe those times were so infrequent!

To cousin Judith, thanks for your caring, wise insights, willingness to share, and enthusiastic support of every book I have written.

Lillian, Ben, Adam, Asher, Rachel, Bryan, Leah, Sandra, Harry, Judie and Jim, and John: You're all valued family, and I am so glad you are out there.

Oi Yin, your loving and resilient spirit deeply moves me and all those around you. You ceaselessly model class, strength, and grace in overcoming adversity. I admire all you give to your two fantastic children.

Ralph, my lifelong friend from kindergarten, as though we are brothers, a better friend does not exist.

Tony and Lillian, thanks for your friendship, caring, and laughs.

One of my best friends is a wonderful man named Ed Washington. More than twenty years ago, at age fourteen, Ed, a very talented athlete, was tackled by three other high school football players. This left Ed a quadriplegic. Although his body is paralyzed, Ed's acceptance, indefatigable optimism, and wonderfully resilient spirit have literally changed my life for the better. Ed inspires me and so many others to be grateful in so many ways. Ed, you are such a determined, optimistic, unbelievable, and classy guy. I love your heart and dignity. What a gift to have you as my friend.

Tracy, thanks for being a great friend and for all your support.

I am deeply indebted to the groundbreaking work of the pioneers in the field of cognitive therapy, Aaron Beck, MD; David Burns, MD; Albert Ellis, PhD; and Martin Seligman, PhD. Their insights and accomplishments helped to inspire this book.

Dr. James Karustis, thanks for your review of Chapter 3 and for the wonderful talks we have during our lunches.

Judy Freed, thanks for your helpful input on the toxic-thought framework as it germinated in my mind.

Thanks to Samuel Knapp of the Pennsylvania Psychological Association for all your wonderful suggestions over the years.

I am very grateful for the support of Katie McHugh, my editor, and all of the caring staff at Perseus Books.

Dr. Dennis O'Hara, without your support, guidance, and wisdom, none of this would have happened. Thank you does not even come close to expressing my gratitude.

Appendix I:
The Nine Toxic-Thought Patterns

"Slow-Burning" Toxic Thoughts

1. *"Always or Never" Trap.* The tendency of parents to think about their kids in either a completely positive or a completely negative manner.

2. *Label Gluing.* In this case, parents affix negative labels to their children, which tend to demotivate their children and inhibit them from making positive changes.

3. *Seething Sarcasm.* Parents are using this toxic form of sarcasm when they deliberately say things that are mocking exaggerations or the opposite of what they're saying through their tone of voice.

4. *Smoldering Suspicions.* Parents prone to smoldering suspicions face major challenges in trusting their children. Ironically, the more children feel they can't be trusted, the less trustworthy they will become.

5. *Detrimental Denial.* Detrimental Denial is a unique type of toxic thought. It reflects parents struggling with denial that their children engage in problematic behaviors.

"Flaring" Toxic Thoughts

6. *Emotional Overheating.* Emotional overheating occurs when a parent convinces herself that her child's behaviors can't be "handled."

7. *Blame Blasting.* Parents who key in on a child and reflexively point their fingers at him are driven by the toxic thought of blame blasting.

8. *"Should" Slamming.* Parents who think about and relate to their children with "you should" statements find that their children will feel distanced, isolated, misunderstood, and resentful.

9. *Dooming Conclusions.* This is a toxic-thinking pattern where parents overly exaggerate the future negative actions and events concerning their children.

Appendix II:
The Toxic-Thought Log

On the following page is a toxic-thought log where you can record your thoughts. The first row includes an example to help guide you. Remember to think of evidence to support your alternative thoughts.

Triggering Event	Type of Toxic Thought	Alternative Thought
"My daughter talked back to me."	"Always or never" trap: "She never shows me any respect."	"She is frustrated and seems to be dumping on me. This does not happen 24/7. I will remind her I don't appreciate her tone and try to determine what is bothering her."

Notes:

It really helps me not to take her so personally when I remind myself how she is struggling.

Resources

The following list of information represents sources of information that may be helpful to parents whose children have various challenges. Please note that several of these sources are Web sites that were active at the time of this writing. Web sites can change or expire on the Internet. Bearing this in mind, not all of those listed below may be active at the time you are reading this book.

ADHD

Attention Research Update
www.helpforadd.com
This Web site will enable you to subscribe to Dr. David Rabiner's free e-mail newsletter, *Attention Research Update,* which helps parents, professionals, and educators stay informed about important new research on ADHD.

Children and Adults with Attention-Deficit/Hyperactivity Disorder (CHADD)
8181 Professional Place, Suite 150
Landover, MD 20785
Toll-free: 800-233-4050
Phone: 301-306-7070
Web site: www.chadd.org

CHADD is a nonprofit organization that offers support to individuals with ADHD and their families, as well as teachers and other professionals.

Anxiety

Anxiety Disorders Association of America (ADAA)
11900 Parklawn Drive, Suite 100
Rockville, MD 20852
Phone: 301-231-9350
Web site: www.adaa.org
The ADAA is a national nonprofit organization dedicated to educating the public, health care professionals, and legislators about the nature and treatment of anxiety disorders.

Depression

Child and Adolescent Bipolar Foundation (CABF)
1187 Wilmette Ave., P.M.B., No. 331
Wilmette, IL 60091
Phone: 847-256-8525
Web site: www.bpkids.org
The CABF is a parent-led nonprofit Web-based membership organization of families raising children diagnosed with, or at risk for, pediatric bipolar disorder.

Depression and Bipolar Support Alliance (DBSA)
730 North Franklin Street, Suite 501
Chicago, IL 60610-7224
Toll-free: 800-826-3632
Web site: www.dbsalliance.org/site/PageServer?pagename=home
The DBSA is a nonprofit organization that provides information, educational materials, programs, exhibits, and media activities about mood disorders.

Depression and Related Affective Disorders Association (DRADA)
Meyer 3-181
600 North Wolfe Street
Baltimore, MD 21287-7381
Phone: 410-955-4647
Web site: www.drada.org
DRADA is an educational organization providing support to individuals affected by a depressive illness, family members, health care professionals, self-help groups, and the general public.

Drugs and Alcohol

The U.S. Department of Health and Human Services
Substance Abuse and Mental Health Services Administration (SAMHSA)
200 Independence Avenue, S.W.
Washington, DC 20201
Toll-free: 877-696-6775
Phone: 202-619-0257
Web site: www.samhsa.gov
SAMHSA works to improve the quality and availability of substance abuse prevention, alcohol and drug addiction treatment, and mental health services.

Learning Disabilities

All Kinds of Minds
1450 Raleigh Road, Suite 200
Chapel Hill, NC 27517
Toll-free: 888-956-4637
Web site: www.Allkindsofminds.org
All Kinds of Minds is a nonprofit institute that provides programs for students with learning disabilities.

International Dyslexia Association (IDA)

8600 LaSalle Road
Chester Building, Suite 382
Baltimore, MD 21286-2044
Toll-free: 800-ABCD-123
Phone: 410-296-0232
Web site: www.interdys.org
The IDA is a nonprofit organization serving individuals with dyslexia, their families, and their communities.

LD OnLine

Web site: www.ldonline.org
LD OnLine seeks to help children and adults reach their full potential by providing accurate and up-to-date information and advice about learning disabilities and ADHD.

Learning Disabilities Association of America

4156 Library Road, Suite 1
Pittsburgh, PA 15234-1349
Phone: 412-341-1515 and 412-341-8077
E-mail: info@ldaamerica.org
Web site: www.ldaamerica.org
The Learning Disabilities Association of America is a nonprofit volunteer organization that advocates for and serves those with learning disabilities, their families, and professionals in the field.

National Center for Learning Disabilities

381 Park Avenue South, Suite 1401
New York, NY 10016
Toll-free: 888-575-7373
Phone: 212-545-7510
Web site: www.ld.org

The mission of the NCLD is to ensure that the nation's 15 million children, adolescents, and adults with learning disabilities have every opportunity to succeed.

National Dissemination Center for Children with Disabilities

P.O. Box 1492
Washington, DC 20013
Toll-free: 800-695-0285
Web site: www.nichcy.org

This organization seems to have changed its name but not its acronym. The Web site states, "NICHCY stands for the National Dissemination Center for Children with Disabilities." NICHCY is a center for information on children and youth with disabilities, laws concerning disabilities, research, and special education.

Office of Special Education and Rehabilitative Services

U.S. Department of Education
400 Maryland Ave., S.W.
Washington, DC 20202-7100
Phone: 202-245-7468
Web site: www.ed.gov/about/offices/list/osers/index.html

By providing funding to programs that serve infants, toddlers, children, and adults with disabilities, OSERS works to ensure that these individuals are not left behind . . . in school, in employment, and in life.

Schwab Learning

Web site: www.SchwabLearning.org

Schwab Learning is a nonprofit organization, dedicated to providing reliable parent-friendly information about learning disabilities from experts and parents.

University of Illinois Extension
Resources for Working with Youth with Special Needs: Learning
Disability
　　Web site: www.urbanext.uiuc.edu/specialneeds/lrndisab.html
　　This Web site provides resources for working with youth who
have special needs.

Organizations with General Child and Teen Mental Health Information

American Psychiatric Association
　　1000 Wilson Boulevard, Suite 1825
　　Arlington, VA 22209-3901
　　Phone: 703-907-7300
　　E-mail: apa@psych.org
　　Web site: www.psych.org
　　The American Psychiatric Association is the main professional
organization of psychiatrists and trainee psychiatrists in the United
States.

American Psychological Association
　　750 First Street, N.E.
　　Washington, DC 20002-4242
　　Toll-free: 800-374-2721
　　Web site: www.apa.org/
　　The American Psychological Association is a scientific and pro-
fessional organization that represents psychologists in the United
States.

Association for Mindfulness in Education
　　Phone: 650-575-5780
　　Web site: www.mindfulness.org
　　Mindfulness-based education is an exciting and important new
development in K–12 education. As a powerful tool to decrease

stress, enhance academic performance, and promote emotional and social well-being, mindfulness is increasingly recognized as an essential support for students, teachers, school administrators, and parents.

Focus Adolescent Services

Phone: 410-341-4216

Web site: www.focusas.com/index.html

Focus Adolescent Services is an Internet clearinghouse of information and resources on teen and family issues to help and support families with troubled and at-risk teens.

National Institute of Child Health and Human Development

National Institutes of Health, DHHS

31 Center Drive, Room 2A32, MSC 2425

Bethesda, MD 20892-2425

Phone: 301-496-5133

Web site: www.nichd.nih.gov

National Institute of Mental Health

National Institutes of Health, DHHS

6001 Executive Boulevard, Room 8184, MSC 9663

Bethesda, MD 20892-9663

Web site: www.nimh.nih.gov

www.WrongPlanet.net

A Web community designed for individuals (and parents of those) with Asperger's syndrome, autism, ADHD, and other pervasive developmental disorders. It provides a forum where members can communicate with each other, an article section where members may read and submit essays or how-to guides about various subjects, and a chat room for real-time communication with others who have Asperger's syndrome.

School Rights

Council of Parent Attorneys and Advocates (COPAA)
P.O. Box 6767
Towson, MD 21285
Phone: 443-451-5270
Web site: www.copaa.net
COPAA is a nonprofit advocacy group of attorneys, nonattorney educational advocates, and parents who are dedicated to securing quality educational services for children with disabilities.

Wrightslaw
Web site: www.Wrightslaw.com
Parents, educators, advocates, and attorneys visit Wrightslaw.com for accurate, reliable information about special-education law and advocacy for children with disabilities. Wrightslaw includes thousands of articles, cases, and free resources about dozens of special-education topics.

Recommended Reading

Barkley, Russell A., PhD. *Taking Charge of ADHD*. New York: Guilford Press, 2000.

Barkley, Russell A., PhD, and Christine M. Benton. *Your Defiant Child*. New York: Guilford Press, 1998.

Bernstein, Jeffrey, PhD. *10 Days to a Less Defiant Child*. New York: Marlowe, 2006.

_____. *10 Days to a Less Distracted Child*. Cambridge, MA: Da Capo Press, 2007.

Brooks, Robert, PhD, and Sam Goldstein, MD. *Raising Resilient Children: Fostering Strength, Hope, and Optimism in Your Child*. New York: McGraw-Hill, 2002.

Canter, Lee. *Homework Without Tears*. New York: HarperCollins, 2005.

Chansky, Tamar. *Freeing Your Child from Negative Thinking*. Cambridge, MA: Da Capo Press, 2008.

Deerwester, Karen. *The Entitlement-Free Child: Positive Parenting Solutions for Raising Confident and Respectful Kids*. Naperville, IL: Sourcebooks, 2009.

Elium, Don, and Jeanne Elium. *Raising a Son*. Berkeley, CA: Celestial Arts, 2004.

Elium, Jeanne, and Don Elium. *Raising a Daughter: Parents and the Awakening of a Healthy Woman*. Berkeley, CA: Celestial Arts, 2003.

Glasser, William. *Choice Theory: A New Psychology of Personal Freedom*. New York: HarperCollins, 1999.

Glasser, William. *Unhappy Teenagers: A Way for Parents and Teachers to Reach Them*. New York: HarperCollins, 2002.

Friedberg, Robert D., and Jessica M. McClure. *Clinical Practice of Cognitive Therapy with Children and Adolescents*. New York: Guilford Press, 2002.

Greene, Ross W. *The Explosive Child*. New York: Harper Paperbacks, 2005.

Hahn, Thich Nhat. *Peace Is Every Step: The Path of Mindfulness in Everyday Life*. New York: Bantam Dell, 2002.

Hallowell, Edward M., and John J. Ratey. *Driven to Distraction*. New York: Touchstone, 1995.

Kraizer, Sherryll. *10 Days to a Bully-Proof Child: The Proven Program to Build Confidence*. Cambridge, MA: Da Capo Press, 2007.

Kurcinka, Mary Sheedy. *Raising Your Spirited Child: A Guide for Parents Whose Child Is More Intense, Sensitive, Perceptive, Persistent, Energetic*. New York: Harper Paperbacks, 1998.

Levine, Mel. *The Myth of Laziness*. New York: Simon and Schuster, 2004.

Mennuti, R. B., A. Freeman, and R. W. Christner. *Cognitive-Behavioral Interventions for Educational Settings: A Handbook for Practice*. Oxford: Routledge, 2006.

Newman, Susan. *Parenting an Only Child: The Joys and Challenges of Raising Your One and Only*. New York: Broadway, 2001.

Nolte, Dorothy Law. *Children Learn What They Live*. New York: Workman, 1998.

Pantley, Elizabeth, and William Sears. *Kid Cooperation: How to Stop Yelling, Nagging, and Pleading and Get Kids to Cooperate*. Oakland: New Harbinger Publications, 1996.

Papolos, Demitri, and J. Papolos. *The Bipolar Child: The Definitive and Reassuring Guide to Childhood's Most Misunderstood Disorder*. 3d ed. New York: Broadway Publishing, 2006.

Power, Thomas J., James L. Karustis, and Dina F. Habboushe. *Homework Success for Children with ADHD: A Family-School Intervention Program.* New York: Guilford Press, 2001.

Rief, Sandra. *The ADHD Book of Lists.* Hoboken: Jossey-Bass, 2003.

Sachs, Brad. *When No One Understands: Letters to a Teenager on Life, Loss, and the Hard Road to Adulthood.* Boston: Trumpeter, 2007.

Samalin, Nancy. *Loving Your Child Is Not Enough: Positive Discipline That Works.* New York: Penguin Books, 1998.

Schaefer, Dick. *Choices and Consequences: What to Do When a Teenager Uses Alcohol/Drugs.* Center City, MN: Hazelton, 1987.

Schwartz, Jeffrey M., and Sharon Begley. *The Mind and the Brain: Neuroplasticity and the Power of Mental Force.* New York: Harper Perennial, 2003.

Seligman, Martin. *The Optimistic Child: Proven Program to Safeguard Children from Depression and Build Lifelong Resilience.* New York: Harper Paperbacks, 1996.

Shariff, Shaheen. *Cyber-Bullying: Issues and Solutions for the School, the Classroom and the Home.* London and New York: Routledge, 2008.

Shaywitz, Sally, MD. *Overcoming Dyslexia.* New York: Alfred A. Knopf, 2003.

Shure, Myrna. *Raising a Thinking Child: Help Your Young Child to Resolve Everyday Conflicts and Get Along with Others.* New York: Pocket Books, 1996.

Taffel, Ron. *The Second Family: Dealing with Peer Power, Pop Culture, the Wall of Silence—and Other Challenges of Raising Today's Teens.* New York: St. Martin's Griffin, 2002.

Taffel, Ron. *Childhood Unbound: Saving Our Kids' Best Selves—Confident Parenting in a World of Change.* New York: Free Press, 2009. Wilens, Timothy E., MD. *Straight Talk About Psychiatric Medications for Kids.* New York: Guilford Press, 1999.

Wright, Pam, and Peter Wright. *From Emotions to Advocacy: The Special Education Survival Guide.* 2d ed. Hartfield, VA: Harbor House Law Press, 2005.

Index

Homosexuality. *See*
Gays/lesbians
Honesty, 143
Hopelessness, 32, 50, 64
Humor, 7, 58, 59
Hygiene, 21
Hypervigilance, 72, 135, 144

Idealistic visions of children
and family life, 10
"If only," use of, 63, 66
"If, then" statements, 177
Illness, 42
Immune system, 81
Inadequacy, 2
In-laws, 83
Insults, 59. *See also* Sarcasm
International Dyslexia
Association (IDA), 230
Internet, 76. *See also*
Computers; Resources;
Web site of author
Intimacy, 26

Journals (personal), xviii, 94–
95. *See also* Writing down
thoughts
Joy, 2, 5, 13, 19, 20, 29, 115,
220
Judgments, 65

Karustis, James, 68

Label gluing, 56–58, 60, 104,
105, 133–138, 152, 178,
209, 223

alternatives to toxic labels,
136(table), 136–137
negative labels as motivators,
138
one's own past label, 134
Last Lecture, The (Pausch), 15
Laziness, 38, 42, 44, 56, 105,
110
LD Online, 230
Learning disabilities, 71, 116,
135, 229–232
Learning Disabilities
Association of America,
230
Legal issues, xiv
Lesbians. *See* Gays/lesbians
Listening, 95, 100. *See also*
under Toxic thoughts
Love, 26, 38, 82, 115, 120,
138, 148, 168, 217. *See
also* Parenting: and
liking/loving children;
Unconditional love

Manipulation, 3, 115, 149
Manners, 199
Mantras, 123
Marijuana, 61, 144. *See also*
Drugs
Marriage issues, 3, 128–129,
149. *See also* Divorce;
Parenting stress: and
marital or couple stress;
Toxic thoughts: and family
relationships
Maturity, 115, 193

University of Illinois
  Extension, 232

Vacations, 96
Values, 69, 171
Video games, 65, 154–155,
  174, 181, 183
Violence. *See* Discipline:
  physical punishment
Vulnerability, 152

Web site of author, 219
Weight issues, 162, 202, 218
Weil, Andrew (MD), 85
Why Can't You Read My Mind?
  (Bernstein), xvi, xviii, 26

Work stress, 82–83
Worrying, 8, 81, 82–83, 84, 91,
  107
Wrightslaw web site, 234
Writing down (as memory
  tool), 90
Writing down thoughts, 37,
  105, 106, 111, 121, 218,
  225–226. *See also* Journals
WrongPlanet.net, 233

Ziglar, Zig, 103

Also available from Dr. Jeffrey Bernstein

10 Days to a Less Defiant Child:
The Breakthrough Program for Overcoming Your Child's Difficult Behavior

A groundbreaking program to help you regain control of your defiant child or teen, including those with Oppositional Defiant Disorder

304 pages • $14.95 paperback
978-1-56924-301-5

10 Days to a Less Distracted Child:
The Breakthrough Program That Gets Your Kids to Listen, Learn, Focus, and Behave

Fresh and effective strategies for helping inattentive children, including those with ADHD and other conditions

336 pages • $14.95 paperback
978-1-60094-019-4

Da Capo Lifelong Books
www.dacapopress.com

Available wherever books are sold